Prehistoric Fish Catches in New Zealand

B. F. Leach and A. S. Boocock

TEMPVS REPARATVM

BAR International Series 584

1993

Published in 2019 by
BAR Publishing, Oxford

BAR International Series 584

Prehistoric Fish Catches in New Zealand

© B. F. Leach and A. S. Boocock, 1993

ISBN 9780860547433 paperback
ISBN 9781407348841 e-book

DOI https://doi.org/10.30861/9780860547433

A catalogue record for this book is available from the British Library

This book is available at www.barpublishing.com

BAR Publishing is the trading name of British Archaeological Reports (Oxford) Ltd.
British Archaeological Reports was first incorporated in 1974 to publish the BAR
Series, International and British. In 1992 Hadrian Books Ltd became part of the BAR
group. This volume was originally published by Tempvs Reparatvm in conjunction
with British Archaeological Reports (Oxford) Ltd / Hadrian Books Ltd, the Series
principal publisher, in 2000. This present volume is published by BAR Publishing,
2019.

BAR
PUBLISHING

BAR titles are available from:

BAR Publishing
122 Banbury Rd, Oxford, OX2 7BP, UK
EMAIL   info@barpublishing.com
PHONE   +44 (0)1865 310431
FAX   +44 (0)1865 316916
www.barpublishing.com

CONTENTS

PROVIDED IN MICROFICHE

The microfiche is available in a digital format at this link:
https://doi.org/10.30861/9780860547433_microfiche

LIST OF TABLES

LIST OF FIGURES

PREFACE AND ACKNOWLEDGEMENTS

The research which forms the basis of this volume began more than 20 years ago during a project of regional archaeology in Palliser Bay, New Zealand. A considerable quantity of fishbone was found in the excavations but there was no established reference material in New Zealand or methodology for its analysis. It was therefore necessary to establish a reference collection of comparative material so that the archaeological fauna could reliably be identified and quantified. The driving force of this work at the time was one of the present authors (Foss Leach) and Atholl Anderson. A systematic method for studying fishbones was formalised at this time which has been followed with very little modification since 1969, and has been extended from New Zealand to the study of tropical Pacific Island economies.

The nature of fishing amongst the Māori people up to the time when European technology was introduced has recently become more than just an academic topic for discussion. The character of pre-European fishing activities now forms part of the basis for negotiations about the extent of modem-day fishing rights of the Māori, guaranteed under the Treaty of Waitangi in 1840. It is therefore important carefully to set down what is known from archaeological evidence, using the most reliable information available. This is what we have set out to do in this volume. The approach taken is to avoid polemic discussion, and set down as much basic factual data as possible. This we have done in an extensive series of tabulated appendices forming a 265 page manuscript provided in microfiche at the end of the volume. The printed text which precedes the microfiche is presented in the form of a summary of the salient features of this evidence, organised around a series of discussion topics. The reason for using a combination of microfiche and printed text was to distribute the full information as inexpensively as possible.

Many people have contributed fishbone collections to this study over the past 20 years, and we would like to thank them for their support and patience. The contributors are too numerous to mention here, but their names are listed in Appendix 2 where the provenance of each assemblage is described.

This project of research would never have been completed without the eamest support of John Yaldwyn, former Director of the National Museum of New Zealand. He gave an enthusiastic boost to the work by establishing a new post of Honorary Curator of Archaeological Fauna and found the funds for building an Archaeozoology Laboratory and associated office and storage space in March 1988. In May and June of the same year the accumulated fishbone identifications (57,711 bones) were entered into the specially designed computer database for Archaeozoology at the National Museum. We would like to thank John Yaldwyn for his foresight in giving formal institutional recognition to Archaeozoology in New Zealand.

The publication of this volume was assisted by a grant from Lottery Science Research, The New Zealand Lottery Grants Board. We would like to express our sincere appreciation for this.

Foss Leach and Angela Boocock
PO Box 26073
Newlands, Wellington
New Zealand
February 24, 1989

INTRODUCTION

In recent years there has been much debate about the nature of fishing activities of the Māori people in their pre-European setting. The debate has been partly fuelled by High Court actions concerning Māori fishing rights, but it is also part of a general increase in interest in traditional Māori affairs. Unfortunately, despite good intentions, not all comments which have been made on the subject of pre-European Māori fishing are very reliable. This is not really surprising because until recently there was very little scientific knowledge of any quality in this field.

Over the past 20 years there has been considerable research effort given to collecting and analysing archaeological fauna both in New Zealand and more generally in the tropical Pacific region. This work has had several focuses:

1: Identifying and describing how humans and their environment adjust to each other (cultural ecology). A special interest here is the human impact on marine resources.

2: Describing ancient diet and nutrition, and how subsistence behaviour is related to this (palaeo-economy).

3: Developing scientific resources for the study of archaeological fauna (archaeozoology). At its simplest level this involves collecting numerous specimens of fish and other animals; at the more complex levels it involves mathematical modelling of the inter-relationship between humans as predators and natural populations.

Unfortunately, very few of these studies have focused directly on fishing as such, and the exceptions have not followed uniform methods of analysis—consequently, it is difficult to compare the results of one study with another. This problem has now been rectified with the re-analysis of numerous prehistoric fishbone collections, using one consistent method (discussed below).

The main objective of this volume is to set down as much factual information as possible which has accumulated from archaeological sites about ancient fish catches in New Zealand, using this single method of analysis of the faunal remains.

Relatively little attention is given to higher level archaeological interpretations of this evidence in this volume. There is ample opportunity for discussion and comparative studies in the forum of short journal publications, but nowhere is there an extensive and reliable body of basic data about prehistoric Māori fish catches on which scholars can draw for this purpose. It is hoped that this volume will provide a suitable body of data to satisfy this need.

We will present this by starting with the more basic information as an extensive appendix, and from this work upwards with summaries by region and different time periods in the main text. Comments that we will make about higher level issues like catch zonation and prehistoric resource management are only tentative because these subjects have not yet been adequately researched.

We also provide some summary observations about sea mammal hunting in prehistoric New Zealand. Recent studies have shown this aspect of the marine food quest to have been of great importance to the pre-European Māori.

The information in this volume leans heavily on two sources of information—the Archaeozoology computer database at the National Museum of New Zealand, and the MA thesis of Angela Boocock (1990). We also provide some summary information from published analyses of fauna in Appendix 9.

Oral History and Archaeology are Complementary

Anthropologists and culture historians are very familiar with the fact that in recording human behaviour there are two dimensions which are important—what people say they do and what people really do in practice. These two categories do not immediately coincide—it is not that humans are inveterate liars, but that our perceptions of our own behaviour are not always as objective as we first think. When anthropologists ask people questions about their behaviour they obtain knowledge which partly relates to belief systems. A good anthropologist not only asks these questions, but also observes what people actually do in practice. The two forms of information are equally important in defining human culture. The structure of beliefs functions like a charter or justification for behaviour.

This distinction between perceived and actual behaviour is very important in the subject of this present report—the traditional fishing of the New Zealand Māori. Until recently, almost all of the knowledge which has accumulated has been of the indirect kind which relates to beliefs and perceptions. It is part of what is more generally called oral history. It is perfectly legitimate and important knowledge, but it is only part of the story which makes up the complete reality. Another important part has been missing until now; this is a record of what fish species were actually being caught, and in what relative numbers, and how this changed in the course of time, and from one region of New Zealand to another. Acquiring this knowledge is purely in the domain of archaeology; that is from studying the scraps of fishbones in the old settlements and midden sites left behind as a permanent record of past behaviour.

This archaeological information is not about belief systems, but is a chronicle of what really did occur in the past. It is well to remember though that there are certain deficiencies in the evidence and scientific problems with interpretation. One of these problems is especially germane to understanding the early culture history of the South Island, and this is a phenomenon known as seasonality. In brief, the early South Island Māori people (whom archaeologists refer to as Archaic New Zealand Polynesians) and their descendants in the late prehistoric and early historic era (whom archaeologists refer to as Classic Māori), had a shifting settlement pattern which has led them to be referred to as 'hunter-gatherers'. For the archaeologist, this poses a special problem in reconstructing a well rounded picture of fishing behaviour and the economy generally, because the evidence from any one archaeological site is merely one piece in a rather complex jigsaw. Frequently, this evidence may be relevant to only one particular season of the year. In order to be sure about what we are studying we therefore need reliable methods for dating the actual season when the settlement was occupied in addition to the normal methods of establishing the age of the site with such techniques as radiocarbon dating. Despite a great deal of research into seasonal dating, we are still sadly deficient in reliable techniques for this purpose.

Extravagant Fishy Folk Tales

In giving sole attention to the archaeological dimension of this subject it is not our intention to imply that information drawn from oral history is in some way less valid than what is presented here. As mentioned above, these two forms of evidence are complementary to each other in providing a realistic picture of past behaviour in its appropriate social setting and held in place by the structure and form of the belief system. It is common for people in thinking about their own society to be quite blind to the differences in these two domains, but perhaps in the field of fishing in particular, European New Zealanders might appreciate the difference more than other aspects of culture. We are all familiar with the notion of the extravagant fish story in European society; indeed the very word 'fish' itself is used to connote something unreliable or not quite right. Phrases like 'fishy' and 'odd-fish' or 'fish-ball' spring to mind. Fishing is one of the most important domains of the apocryphal story—however, twentieth century European fishermen have no monopoly on fishy folk tales. Baucke once remarked that the Moriori of the Chatham Islands excelled in the art of fishing for lobsters, and that:

> "a diver who appeared with three—one in each hand, and one held by the antennae between the teeth, was acclaimed *tchim' tchakat' me' kye*" (Skinner and Baucke, 1928:360).

This curious phrase from the incompletely recorded Moriori language is thought to be equivalent to the Polynesian "*tenei tangata mahi kai*"—meaning a 'food provider of renown' (Dave Simmons, 1976: pers.comm.). Like any good fishing story, it only just stretches credulity.

There are many reasons why people are inclined to tell tall stories about fishing behaviour. One of them is that it is often rather difficult to check up on the truth of the story, especially about the 'one that got away'. It is also an area requiring expert knowledge and skills and in many Pacific island societies, especially Polynesian ones, personal standing and mana are closely associated with one's performance as a fisherman. It is hardly surprising that when a fisherman returns from a day's fishing at sea he proudly displays only the prestigious portion of the catch for public view and is inclined to keep less noteworthy species in the canoe. An anthropologist asking fishermen about their catches gets a very biased account of the real situation. It is also not in the best interests of any fisherman to give away too much of his knowledge to someone else about fishing methods, the best places and times to catch certain kinds of fish, or even where his catches of the day have been made. One of us (Leach) has spent a considerable amount of time collecting modern knowledge about Polynesian fishing and been told many times that to give away knowledge is to give away power—yet another reason why fishermen not only withhold knowledge but positively divert the listener from the truth. It has been shown by Fleming (1986:109–115) that even high ranking chiefs may be kept ignorant of matters relating to fishing. A detailed case has been made elsewhere (Leach and Davidson, 1988) about the amount of caution required when using ethnographic accounts or oral history for the purpose of understanding the fishing behaviour of communities immediately before the historic era. As earlier mentioned, an amalgamation of historic and archaeological data is required if a reliable account is to be made.

The Importance of Fishing in Offshore Waters

A very clear distinction can be made between two categories of fish and fishing in pre-European Polynesian society—those that enhance the prestige of the fisherman and those that do not. Fish that are common and easy to catch are not especially sought after, while fish that are difficult to catch and involve a degree of danger are highly sought after. There is now a wealth of archaeological evidence for the Pacific region including New Zealand that the species which were highly sought after were generally caught in only small numbers. Despite this, a disproportionate amount of the ethnohistoric record is devoted to these species. In this respect there are clear similarities between the tropical and temperate parts of the Pacific.

The mundane type of fish in the tropics is quite clearly the parrotfish of the Scaridae family. In temperate New Zealand the comparable type is the wrasse of the Labridae family. There are other types of fish which fit into these categories, but these are the most notable examples. They are very easy to catch, in shallow inshore waters. There are very few myths and legends about

them, fishermen don't talk about them very much, yet they catch them in great number. They are very important in household economics.

The types of fish that have prestige are invariably the fast swimming predatory pelagic fish which are generally caught at the surface over deep offshore waters. The more danger associated with a species, the more prestige results from catching one. Species common to both tropical and temperate Pacific waters which fall into this category are:

Marlin/Swordfish	-	Istiophoridae/Xiphiidae
Dolphinfish	-	Coryphaenidae
Tuna	-	Thunnidae/Katsuwonidae
Barracouta	-	Gempylidae/Sphyraenidae

With the exception of barracouta, the presence of bones of these fish in archaeological sites is a clear indication that people were putting to sea to pit their wits against an adversary worthy of an expert fisherman. The exception, the barracouta, is seasonally abundant in shallow waters in some parts of New Zealand.

So far as is known, only in the Mariana islands did people regularly catch marlin/swordfish and dolphinfish in the Pacific region in the prehistoric era (Leach and Fleming et al., 1988). Bones of tuna are very rare, but one or two cases are known where fishermen were skilled in their capture (Leach and Intoh et al., 1984). Not one bone of any of these species has ever been found in a New Zealand archaeological site although, as will be seen below, barracouta bones are very common.

The accumulated evidence clearly shows that offshore fishing resulted in a very small harvest. Despite this there is an equally impressive body of evidence that for some communities it was socially very important. In a nutshell, offshore fishing was almost always of great cultural significance, but seldom had any economic value.

SCIENTIFIC METHODS USED FOR ANALYSIS OF ARCHAEOLOGICAL FISHBONES

The methods used for the analysis of archaeological fishbones in New Zealand and the Pacific have been fully described elsewhere (Leach, 1976; Leach and Davidson, 1977; Leach and Ward, 1981), so only a few details need be given here.

There are two basic units which are important in the analysis of archaeological fauna and these need to be carefully defined—these are the 'Assemblage' and the 'Minimum Number of Individuals' or MNI.

An assemblage is defined as any single excavation unit. Thus, all bone from one excavation square (usually one metre square) and one excavation level is designated as an assemblage.

The Minimum Number of Individuals (abbreviated as MNI) is defined as the smallest number of individuals which is necessary to account for all of the skeletal elements of a species in a faunal assemblage (Smith, 1985:107). MNI are calculated with reference to a single assemblage unit. There are other ways of calculating the relative abundance of species from faunal material, such as the weight of bone, or the Number of Identified Specimens (NISP), or the Minimum Number of Elements (MNE). The issue of which unit is the best choice has evoked much debate, some of which borders on the hysterical. This is not the place to enter this foray; we merely note that the unit of abundance used here is the MNI.

In order to understand something of the character of ancient fishing behaviour and the impact which people have on their surrounding environment, the first aim of faunal analysis is to produce a list of MNI for each species for each assemblage. The next step is to combine these lists in various ways in order to examine changes in time and space. Changes in the relative abundance of species in prehistoric catches can be due to several possible causes:

Seasonal changes in natural abundance
Long term effects of human predation
Changes in human behaviour

Of these, the most studied so far relate to changes in human behaviour—that is, cultural changes. A change in technology, for example, such as more widespread use of nets, results in dramatic changes in the character of fish catches. By taking into account seasonal evidence at settlements, archaeologists are able to reconstruct a very detailed picture of the yearly round of economic behaviour of ancient societies.

It is worth noting that for the purposes of this present volume, large numbers of assemblages are added together, smearing over this fine seasonal detail. There are certain dangers in trying to paint a picture with such a broad brush, but this is unavoidable here. There is increasing interest in the effects of human predation on natural distributions and abundance, and archaeological methods are still being developed in this field.

During analysis each assemblage is sorted into identifiable and not identifiable bones, and then re-bagged. The identifiable fragments are then sorted into five anatomical groups (See Figures 1 and 2), and again re-bagged. Taking each part of the anatomy in turn, bones are then sorted into species/genera/families, and identified with reference to a comparative collection, containing mounted and boxed bones. All information is then entered into a computer database which has been specifically developed for fish bone studies in the Pacific region (see Leach 1986), and is kept in the National Museum of New Zealand. A few bones are sometimes found which cannot be matched in the comparative collection, even to family level, and these are entered as Species A, Species B, etc., and appear in summary tables in the category 'Teleostomi'.

Developing comparative material for these studies is a very large undertaking because ideally over 100 specimens is required for each species for measurements to be made for the reconstruction of live animal characteristics from bones. The present collection we use for the Pacific region including New Zealand consists of over 300 species, which is about one third of those which could be found in archaeological sites. Only about 50 of these are at all likely in New Zealand sites. Although the comparative collection is reasonably satisfactory, identifications from bones are not always certain. For this reason, all identifications should be understood as meaning that the bone involved is most similar to the nominated species amongst the choices available. A formal way of expressing this is to say that an identification of "*Conger verreauxi*" should be understood as meaning "cf. *Conger verreauxi*".

A full list of taxonomic binomials and their equivalent common names of the main fishes identified in New Zealand archaeological sites is provided in Appendix 1.

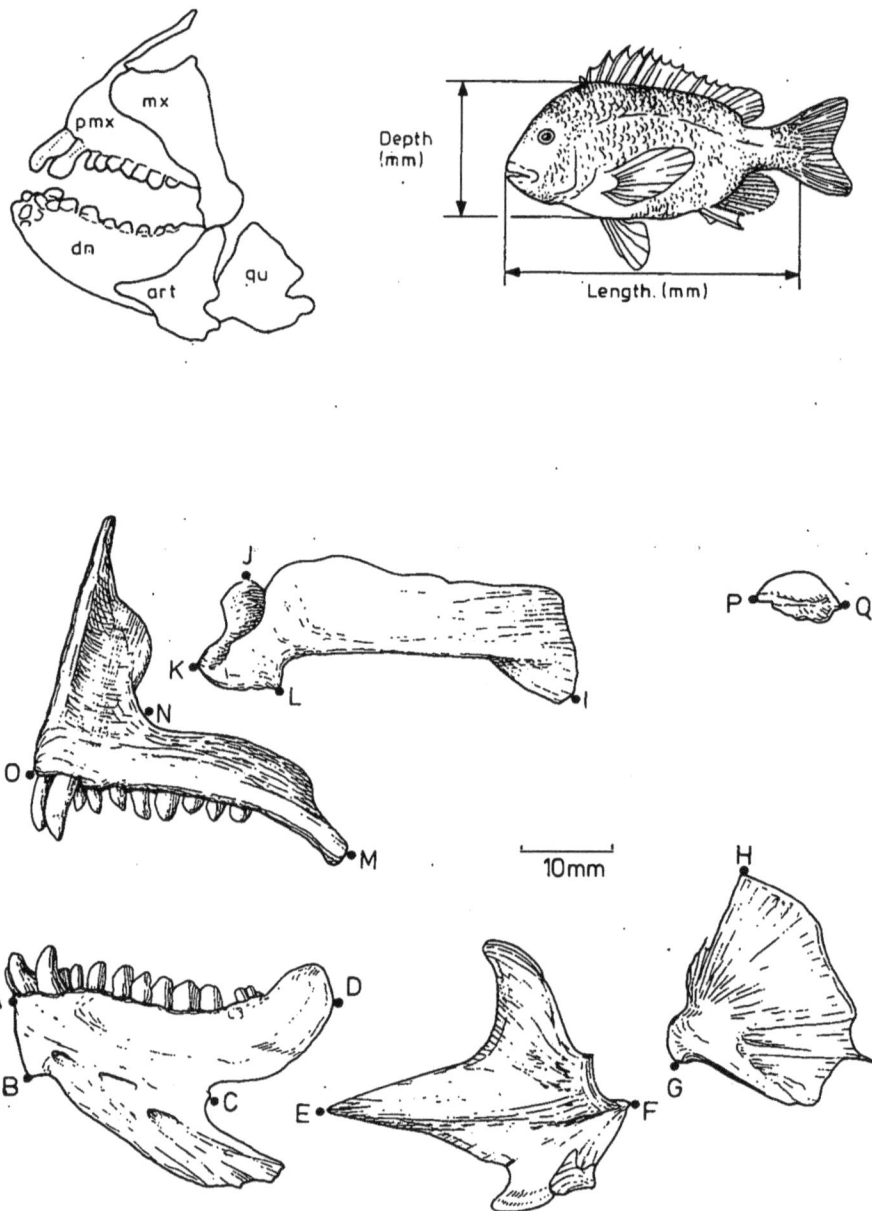

Figure 1: Five Paired Fish Cranial Bones Normally Identified. The bones identified are—in the upper jaw the premaxilla (*pmx*) and maxilla (*mx*), and in the lower jaw the dentary (*dn*), articular (*art*) and quadrate (*qu*) (see Leach 1986). In the top right is shown the otolith, another anatomical element frequently found in archaeological sites which can be used for seasonal dating. Apart from these, there are numerous 'special' bones which are also identified by archaeologists (see Figure 2). Anatomical landmarks are also illustrated. These are used for measurements for the purposes of reconstructing live animal length and weight in order to evaluate prehistoric fish catch characteristics (Boocock 1986).

Fortunately, archaeologists are now taking much more notice of fish bones, and there is increasing standardization in methodology through the efforts of the International Council of Archaeozoology (ICAZ) and publications on cranial anatomy and methods of measurement (Casteel, 1976; Desse-Berset, 1984; Izquierdo, 1988; Cannon,

1987; Courtemanche and Legendre, 1985). An atlas of cranial anatomy for New Zealand archaeologists will be published shortly (Leach n.d.).

Since we are not personally responsible for all fish bone identifications which have ever been

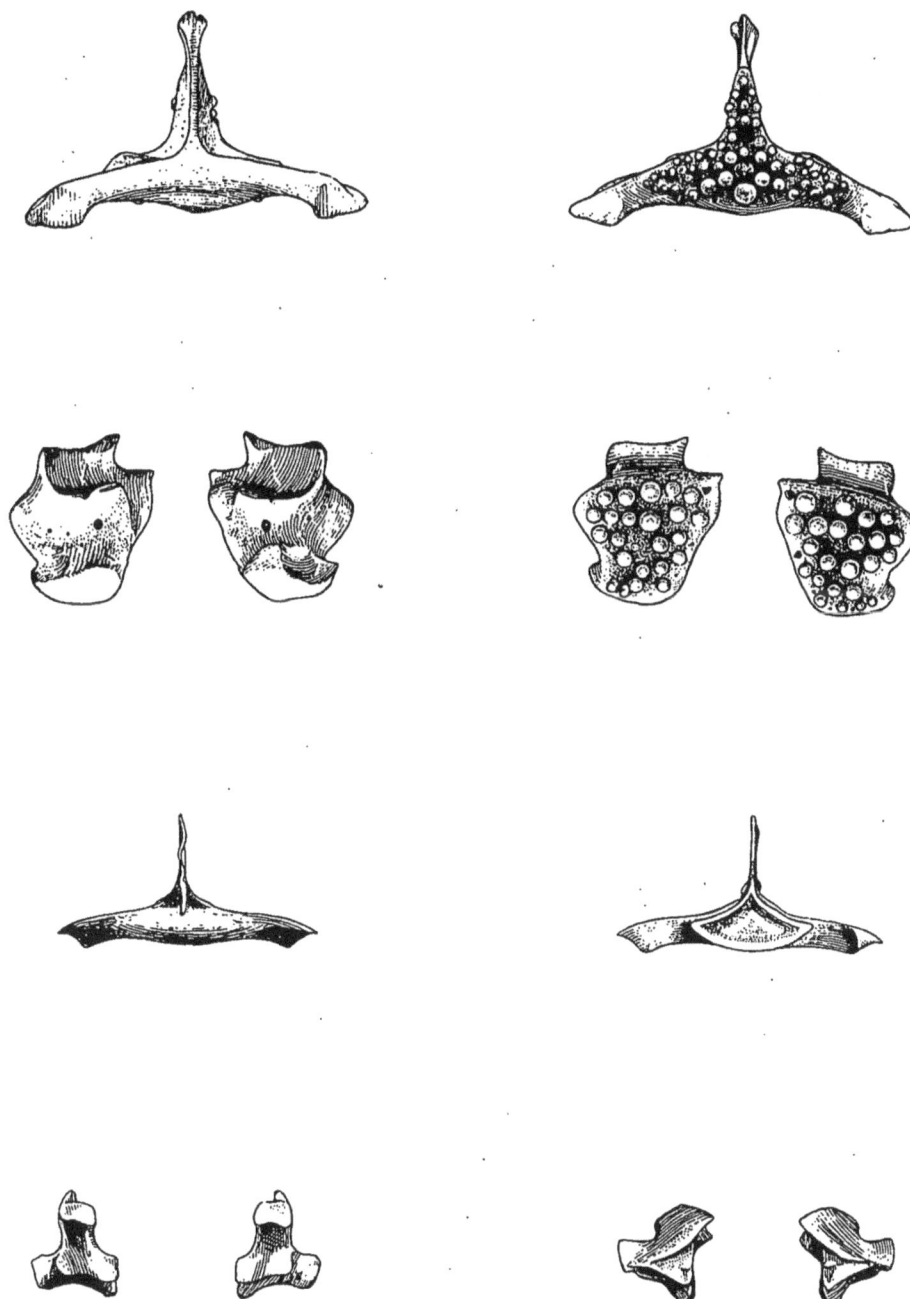

Figure 2: Selection of 'Special' Bones used for Identification. These are pharyngeal bones and are very distinctive of different species. They are common in New Zealand archaeological sites (see Leach and Anderson, 1979).

done in New Zealand we cannot be sure that all published results are equally reliable. Moreover, the methods followed in calculation of MNI are not standard amongst archaeologists. For this reason, in this volume we have clearly divided any results into those for which we are personally responsible (Appendices 2–8), and those for which we are not (Appendix 9). Summary comments on catches by region and at different periods are based on our own data unless otherwise stated.

It may be noticed in some of the tables with binomial names that the names are incomplete. This is because we have arbitrarily truncated s names at 20 characters for printing purposes. There should be no ambiguity as to what species is referred to. The full names are specified in the glossary (Appendix 1).

BASIC INFORMATION ON PREHISTORIC FISH CATCHES IN NEW ZEALAND

An important source of information about fish catches of the pre-European Māori is the published accounts by archaeologists who have carried out research in this field. However, as explained above, not all of this is equally reliable or directly comparable between studies. It has been argued in several publications that there is a need to standardize our techniques, and with

Table 138: Identified Fishbones for Different Anatomy		

Anatomy	Number of Bones		
	Left	Right	Total
Premaxilla	6659	6574	13233
Dentary	6424	6296	12720
Maxilla	5137	5112	10249
Quadrate	4624	4631	9255
Articular	4571	4600	9171
Special Bones			3083
Inferior Pharyngeal	1307		
Right Sup.Pharyngeal	245		
Left Sup. Pharyngeal	245		
Vomer	26		
Operculum	512		
Dorsal/Erect. Spine	70		
Dorsal Spine Cage	30		
Wing Hook	2		
Caudal Peduncle	4		
Vertebra	642		
Number of Bones	**3083**		**57711**

this in mind a computer database has been established at the National Museum of New Zealand and many previously studied archaeological fishbone collections have been completely re-analyzed. The basic data from this research is given in Appendices 2 to 8.

Many sites have not been re-analyzed yet, but for various reasons we consider the MNI to be reasonably trustworthy for 21 for which there is published information. Basic data on these are given in Appendix 9. However, in the summary comments in this volume, these 'other MNI' are not included.

Sixty-three sites have been restudied so far using carefully standardized techniques, and the location of these is shown in Figures 3, 4 and 5. Fifteen of these are in the North Island, 43 in the South island, and five in the Chatham Islands.

Before discussing the salient features of the fishbone assemblages some comments should be made about the appendices. Different archaeologists use quite different methods of curating material from their excavations, and the range of ways of referring to time/space provenances (assemblages) is therefore diverse. It is necessary to follow some standard method of referring to space/time units for this present analysis, and the details of this are provided in Appendix 2. In all of the tabulated material which follows, any particular assemblage is referred to using two simple numbers which represent the space and time reference numbers respectively. For example, 1,1 refers to space unit 1 and time unit 1. If Appendix 2 is consulted, it will be seen that Space unit 1 is Breaksea Sound Site 1 Trench A. Time unit 1 is Layer 6Eb. The space units are also given an acronym, in this case BRE1001 (BRE1 = Breaksea Sound Site 1, and 001 = the area within the site, which is Trench A). There is a total of 608 discrete space units, and 1000 space/time units (assemblages).

At the beginning of Appendix 8 we provide a clearly worked example of how to decode the assemblage reference numbers used here so as to be able to refer back to the original archaeological provenance using the terminology of the archaeologist who catalogued the bags from the excavation in the first place.

The information describing the number of assemblages in each site, and the number of bones in each square of each site, is given in Appendices 3, 4 and 5. An indication of antiquity for each of the 1000 assemblages and the basis for these assessments is given in Appendix 6, and the regional category of each site in Appendix 7.

Finally, the MNI for each of the 1000 assemblages is given in Appendix 8 (Tables 1–118) and for the previously published, but not re-analysed assemblages, in Appendix 9 (Tables 119–137). These tables are organised around the individual archaeological sites, and in many cases a site requires more than one set of tables because the large number of space/time units could not be accommodated by the maximum number of columns which could be printed across the page. For each set of tables the information is given in four parts—the matrix of MNI for each assemblage, and the totals, for both the individual taxon identified, and for each fish family.

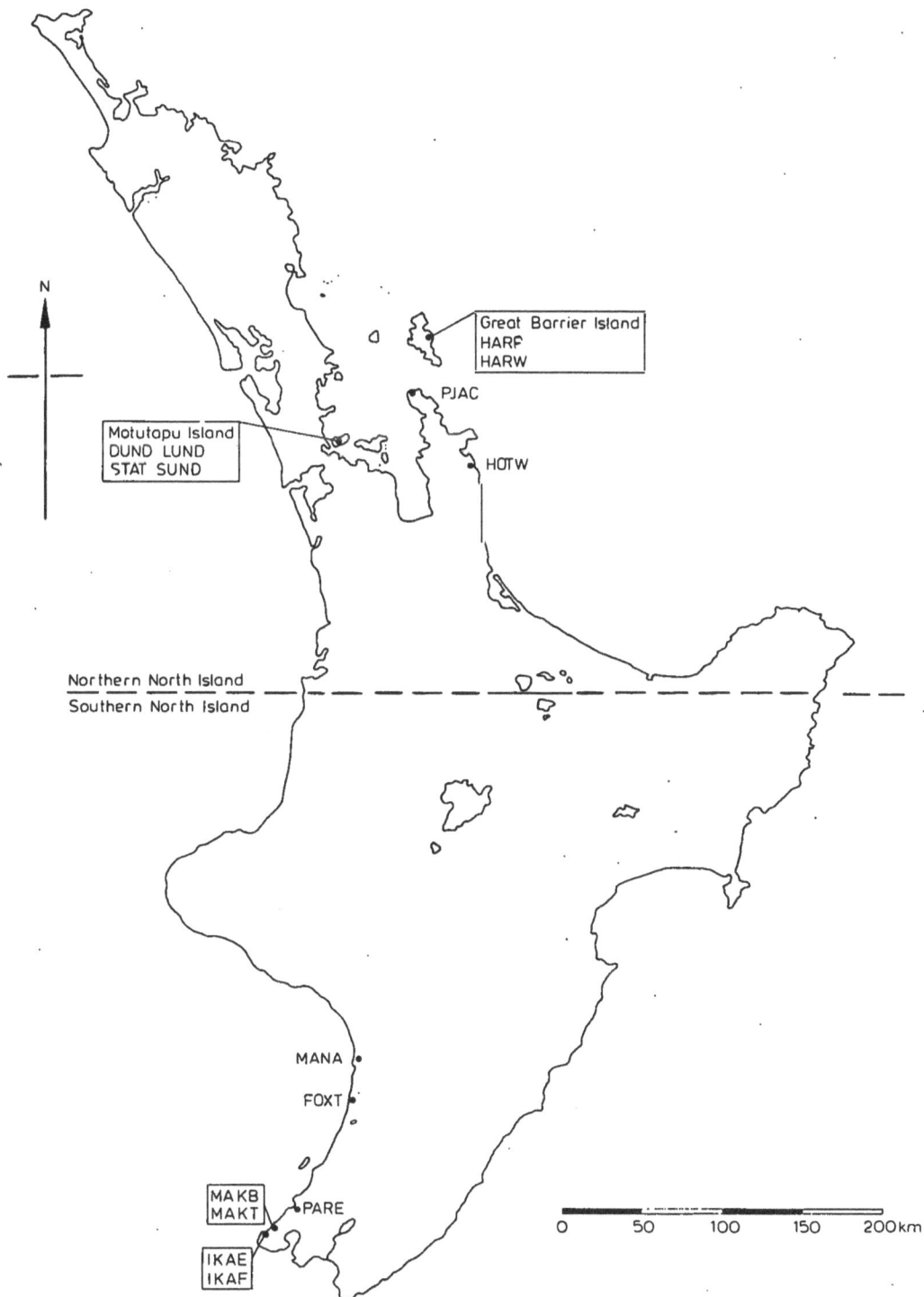

Figure 3: Archaeological Sites Examined from the North Island. The 15 archaeological sites studied are listed in Table 139.

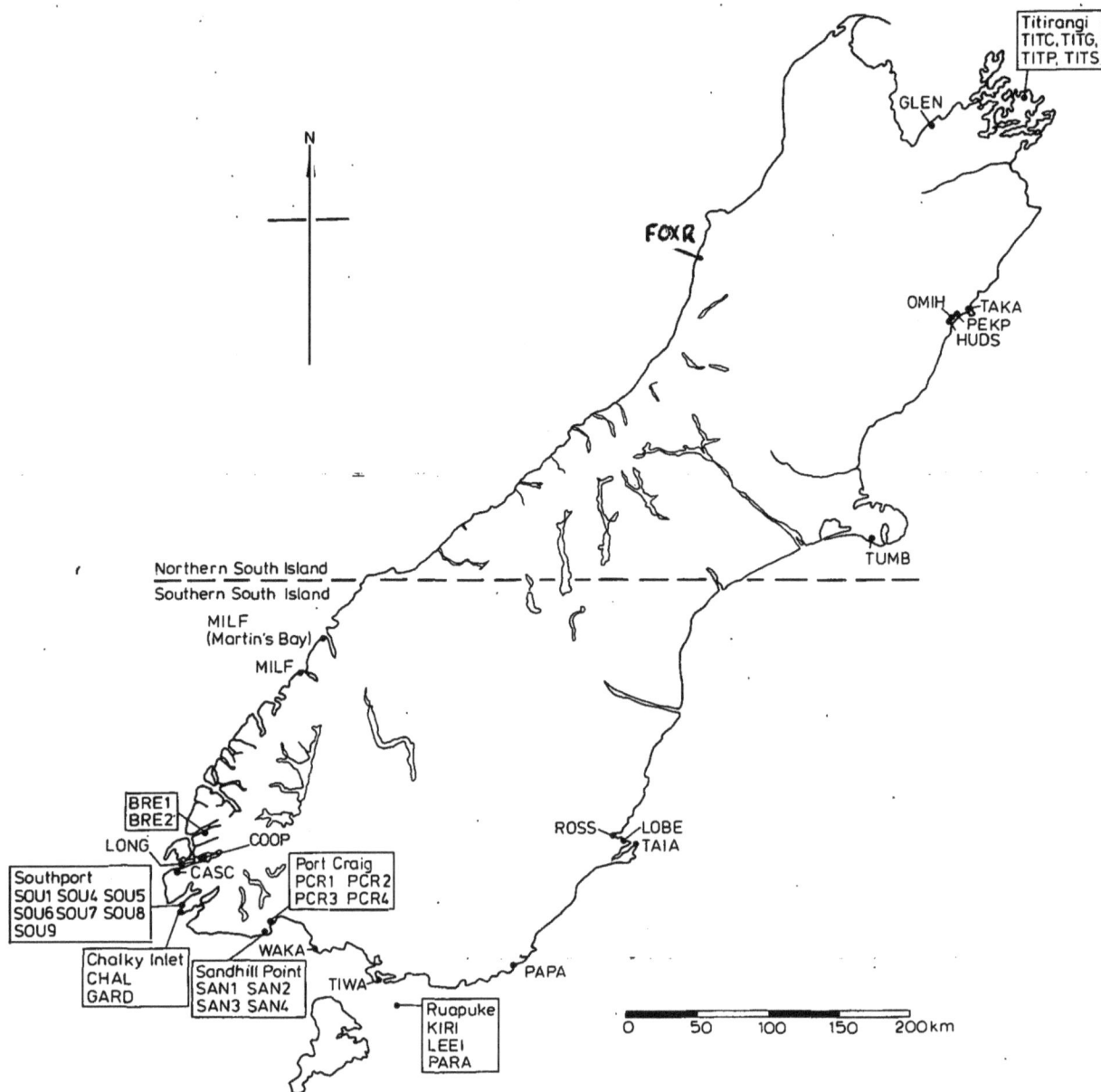

Figure 4: Archaeological Sites Examined from the South Island. The 43 archaeological sites studied are listed in Table 139.

These tables permit various kinds of second tier research to be carried out—for instance analysis of changes through time in each site, and a study of variation in the spatial distribution within each site. These fine grained studies are beyond the scope of this volume.

A summary of MNI for the 84 archaeological sites is provided in Table 139. This shows that we have information from a total catch of 30,017 fish from New Zealand archaeological sites. Just under half of these (12,393) result from the recent re-study, and represent a good sample from which to define the broad picture of fishing in early New Zealand. Table 138 shows the numbers of bones identified for different parts of the cranial anatomy.

These 57,711 identified fish bones come from exactly 1000 different archaeological

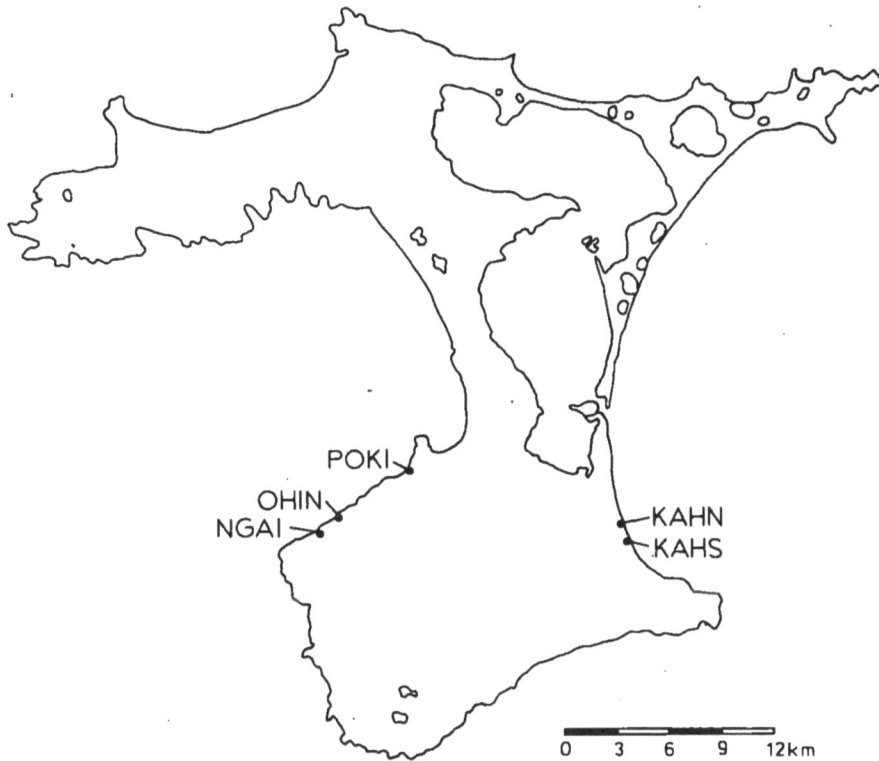

Figure 5: Archaeological Sites Examined from the Chatham Islands. The five archaeological sites studied are listed in Table 139.

assemblages, which have discrete status in time and space. An overall summary of Māori fish catches is provided in Tables 141 and 142. These give a clear indication of the relative abundance of different types of fish, first with reference to the taxonomic units relevant to the basic identification, and then organized by fish family. The percentage values are average percentages for each assemblage. This method of working out summary percentages is therefore not biased towards the composition of larger assemblages of bones, but produces unweighted percentages. The reader would find it difficult to re-calculate and verify any one percentage from the MNI figures given below, although these could be verified using the full data set in the Appendices. Programs which service the database do these calculations automatically. As new data is entered into the database, or refined identifications made of old material, re-calculation of statistics is also automatic.

The prehistoric Māori people of New Zealand caught marine fish from 27 different families, but

all but eight of these were less than 1% of an average catch, and were therefore of only minor economic importance. These eight numerically important fish are shown in Table 140.

It is important to realise that although there is no statistical bias in favour of larger assemblages, there is a clear bias towards results from the South Island. This is because two thirds of the sites studied are from the South island. It would be possible to work out weighted mean values as an alternative to the figures above, but this is not very satisfactory because the regional differences are very large, and we would end up with figures which are not typical of any region. This type of problem is well understood by statisticians, but not always by archaeologists, or those using archaeological information to study the past. We wish to emphasise as strongly as possible our view that regional differences in the culture of prehistoric New Zealand are so profound that New Zealand wide summaries can be either misleading or invalid. The summary presented in

15

Table 139: Checklist of Archaeological Sites

List of 84 sites for which there is reliable information on relative numbers of fish species taken by pre-European Māori fishermen in New Zealand. Sixty-three of these sites have been totally re-studied using strictly comparable methods, and data entered into the National Museum computer database.

NZAA No = New Zealand Archaeological Site Reference Number.
NOTC = Not Coded in National Museum database, but fish data published in archaeological reports.
MNI1 = Previously published MNI considered reasonably reliable. Those which are asterisked (*) were supervised by Leach.
MNI2 = MNI from National Museum database.

Site Name	Abbrev.	NZAA No	Region	MNI1	MNI2
Andrewburn, Fiordland	NOTC	S?	Sthrn South Is	9	-
Breaksea Sound 1	BRE1	S148/3	Sthrn South Is	-	1153
Breaksea Sound 2	BRE2	S148/5	Sthrn South Is	-	1
Cascade Cove	CASC	S156/3	Sthrn South Is	-	125
CHA	NOTC	C240/	Chatham Is	884	-
Chalky Island	CHAL	S165/31	Sthrn South Is	-	45
CHB	NOTC	C240/	Chatham Is	4978	-
CHC	NOTC	C240/	Chatham Is	3	-
Coopers Island	COOP	S157/5	Sthrn South Is	-	219
Davidson Undefended Site	DUND	N38/37	Nthrn North Is	-	54
Fox River	FOXR	S37/1	Nthrn South Is	-	102
Foxton	FOXT	N148/1	Sthrn North Is	-	270
Mount Camel, Houhora	NOTC	N6/4	Nthrn North Is	2542	-
Garden Island	GARD	S165/32	Sthrn South Is	-	1
Goose Bay Midden	TITG	S16/104	Nthrn South Is	-	2
Harataonga Bay East	NOTC	N30/4	Nthrn North Is	231	-
Harataonga Bay Pa	HARP	N30/3	Nthrn North Is	-	7
Harataonga Bay West	HARW	N30/5	Nthrn North Is	-	65
Hot Water Beach	HOTW	N44/69	Nthrn North Is	-	278
Hudson's Site	HUDS	S49/75	Nthrn South Is	-	27
Huriawa Peninsula	NOTC	S155/1	Sthrn South Is	414	-
Kahiti North	KAHN	C240/21	Chatham Is	41*	95
Kahiti South	KAHS	C240/20	Chatham Is	77*	159
Kellys Beach, Stewart Is	NOTC	S?	Sthrn South Is	13	-
Leahy Undefended Site	LUND	N38/30	Nthrn North Is	-	12
Lee Island	LEEI	S187/11	Sthrn South Is	-	8
Long Beach	LOBE	S164/20	Sthrn South Is	-	5770
Long Island	LONG	S156/1	Sthrn South Is	-	252
Makara Beach Midden	MAKB	N160/105	Sthrn North Is	-	50
Makara Terrace Midden	MAKT	N160/106	Sthrn North Is	-	24
Milford	MILF	Unknown	Sthrn South Is	-	7
Ohinemamao	OHIN	C240/273	Chatham Is	2*	17
Old Pier (Avoca) Point	NOTC	S49/46	Nthrn South Is	25*	-
Omihi	OMIH	S49/37	Nthrn South Is	-	118
Omimi, Otago	NOTC	S155/31	Sthrn South Is	27	-
Otokia Mouth, Brighton	NOTC	S?	Sthrn South Is	3	-
Papatowai	PAPA	S184/5	Sthrn South Is	-	27
Parangiaio	PARA	S187/9	Sthrn South Is	-	12
Paremata	PARE	N160/50	Sthrn North Is	-	147
Parewanui Midden	MANA	N148/55	Sthrn North Is	-	54
Peketa Pa	PEKP	S49/23	Nthrn South Is	-	54
Pokiakio	POKI	C240/266	Chatham Is	2*	7
Port Craig 1	PCR1	S175/71	Sthrn South Is	-	114
Port Craig 2	PCR2	S175/72	Sthrn South Is	-	2
Port Craig 3	PCR3	S175/73	Sthrn South Is	-	1
Port Craig 4	PCR4	S175/74	Sthrn South Is	-	28

Continued on next page

Table 140 should therefore be viewed with considerable caution.

REGIONAL VARIATION IN FISH CATCH COMPOSITION

The details from the 63 archaeological sites can be grouped together into a small number of zones to give some indication of regional variation. It is well known from archaeological studies that human culture greatly varied throughout New Zealand, indeed this is a constant theme in recent publications (e.g. Davidson, 1984).

For this purpose, five regions were chosen—northern and southern North Island, northern and southern South Island, and Chatham Islands. The lines of demarcation (See Figures 3,4,5) are semi-arbitrary and not very important because archaeological sites which have been examined clearly fall into such groups. The data are given as MNI and % values both for the identified taxa and for fish families in Tables 143 to 146.

Table 139 Continued					
Port Jackson	PJAC	N35/88	Nthrn North Is	-	45
Pounawea, Otago	NOTC	S148/1	Sthrn South Is	430	-
Purakanui Inlet	NOTC	S164/18	Sthrn South Is	2745	-
Riverton	NOTC	S176/1	Sthrn South Is	14*	-
Ross Rocks	ROSS	S155/38	Sthrn South Is	-	144
Rotokura	NOTC	S14/1	Nthrn South Is	585*	-
Sandhill Point 1	SAN1	S175/10	Sthrn South Is	-	214
Sandhill Point 2	SAN2	S175/10	Sthrn South Is	-	2
Sandhill Point 3	SAN3	S175/10	Sthrn South Is	-	364
Sandhill Point 4	SAN4	S175/10	Sthrn South Is	-	105
Slipper Is, Coromandel	NOTC	N?	Nthrn North Is	13	-
Southport 1	SOU1	S165/20	Sthrn South Is	-	443
Southport 4	SOU4	S165/23	Sthrn South Is	-	86
Southport 5	SOU5	S165/24	Sthrn South Is	-	120
Southport 6	SOU6	S165/25	Sthrn South Is	-	185
Southport 7	SOU7	S165/26	Sthrn South Is	-	111
Southport 8	SOU8	S165/27	Sthrn South Is	-	10
Southport 9	SOU9	S165/28	Sthrn South Is	-	1
Station Bay Pa	STAT	N38/25	Nthrn North Is	-	156
Sunde Site	SUND	N38/24	Nthrn North Is	-	128
Taiaroa Head	TAIA	S164/191	Sthrn South Is	-	40
Tairua, Coromandel	NOTC	N44/2	Nthrn North Is	70*	-
Takahanga Midden (PO)	TAKA	S49/13	Nthrn South Is	-	130
Te Ika a Maru, East	IKAE	N164/16	Sthrn North Is	-	63
Te Ika a Maru, Pa	IKAF	N164/22	Sthrn North Is	-	199
Te Kiri Kiri	KIRI	S187/5	Sthrn South Is	-	56
Te Ngaio	NGAI	C240/277	Chatham Is	5*	4
The Glen	GLEN	S14/20	Nthrn South Is	-	179
Titirangi Cattleyards	TITC	S16/92	Nthrn South Is	-	14
Titirangi Pa	TITP	S16/93	Nthrn South Is	-	1
Titirangi Sandhills	TITS	S16/83	Nthrn South Is	-	47
Tiwai Point	TIWA	S181/16	Sthrn South Is	-	103
Tumbledown Bay	TUMB	S94/30	Sthrn South Is	-	42
Waianakarua Mouth	NOTC	S?	Sthrn South Is	4	-
Waihora	NOTC	C240/283	Chatham Is	4197	-
Wakapatu	WAKA	S176/4	Sthrn South Is	-	94
Washpool Midden	NOTC	N168/22	Sthrn North Is	431*	-
Whangamata Wharf	NOTC	N49/2	Nthrn North Is	6	-
Totals				**17751**	**12393**
Total for duplicates				127	302
Nett MNI				**17624**	**12091**
Combined Total					**29715**
Adjustment for duplicates					302
Total Fish MNI from 84 Archaeological Sites					**30017**

It was earlier noted that fish from only eight families appeared with abundances greater than 1% of catches. When the information is looked at with finer detail by region this number increases to 19 families (ignoring unreliable evidence of cartilaginous fish—see Table 147). This is a clear indication of the importance of regional cultural differences in New Zealand. The patterns of course also reflect changes in natural abundance of different fishes about the coastal waters of New Zealand.

VARIATION THROUGH TIME IN FISH CATCH COMPOSITION

In order to try and document changes in fish catches over archaeological time the individual assemblages must be assigned to age categories. The details of this are explained in Appendix 6. In brief, not all assemblages can be reliably placed in time. However, if we consider three broad age categories which are widely used by New Zealand archaeologists, there is reasonable confidence in most cases. There is generally little doubt when a context is Post-European in age because there are often historic records relating to a site. Archaeologists frequently use the term Archaic to refer to sites which show distinct evidence of moa exploitation, or have dates before about AD 1500, or have cultural features which show the Pacific island affiliations of the New Zealand Polynesian inhabitants. Finally, the term Classic Māori is used to refer to archaeological sites which are closer to the culture of the historically recorded Māori people.

When the fish catches are grouped into these three categories, any patterns of change through time should be evident. This is done by both MNI and % of catch for both identification taxa and fish families in Tables 148 to 151.

When the basic fish catches were described it was noted that the evidence is heavily biased towards South island archaeological sites. This same point must be made here. Any chronological changes which are observed are weighted towards events over time in the South island. However, there is another complicating factor too. Far more Archaic assemblages are from the South island, and far more Classic Māori assemblages are from the North island.

Despite these biases, there are some dramatic changes in fish catch composition over time. The most notable of these are indicated in the summary chart provided below. The first four species show a dramatic decline in importance (barracouta, red cod, snapper, ling), and the remaining six species show dramatically increased importance over time (conger eel, freshwater eel, tarakihi, sea perch, blue cod, and spotty).

Summary of Changes in % Abundance over Time

Taxon	Early	Middle	Late
Thyrsites atun	62.43	37.07	7.97
Pseudophycis bachus	11.25	10.08	4.77
Chrysophrys auratus	8.30	8.93	1.40
Genypterus blacodes	3.91	3.39	1.96
Conger verreauxi	0.24	0.99	1.01
Anguilla sp.	0.01	0.89	1.63
Nemadactylus macropterus	0.49	4.57	6.51
Scorpaenidae	0.77	4.70	9.71
Parapercis colias	3.02	7.10	14.14
Pseudolabrus sp.	4.97	9.79	44.39

FISHING FOR CRAYFISH IN EARLY NEW ZEALAND

The remains of crayfish from archaeological sites may be identified by the mandibles which are quite dense and in optimum soil chemical conditions readily survive. Conditions which

Table 140: Eight Fish Numerically Important to the Pre-European Māori

Family	Common Name	%
Gempylidae	barracouta	46.8
Labridae	largely spotty	12.1
Moridae	largely red cod	10.0
Sparidae	snapper	7.5
Mugiloididae	blue cod	5.9
Ophidiidae	ling	3.5
Scorpaenidae	sea perch	3.4
Cheilodactylidae	largely tarakihi	2.6

favour survival are alkaline soils, such as ash layers and shell middens. Unfortunately, lack of knowledge on the part of archaeologists as to what these fragments look like has resulted in many being discarded as shell fragments in the past. More careful studies of middens have revealed large numbers of these mandibles (see Table 152). These have been used to reconstruct the live size of crayfish caught by pre-European Māori people (Leach and Anderson, 1979), and this shows a dramatic lowering of size over centuries. This is further discussed under 'resource management' below.

So far, only the common rock lobster, *Jasus edwardsii*, has been found archaeologically. The mandibles of the much larger species known as the packhorse crayfish, *Jasus verreauxi* are quite distinctive, and it is surprising that none of these have been found. Since it has a more northern distribution, it may eventually be found in northern sites when better quality midden analysis is carried out. The freshwater crayfish, *Paranephrops planifrons* and *P. zealandicus* also have distinctive mandibles, but again these have not yet been found archaeologically.

PROBLEMS OF ARCHAEOLOGICAL SURVIVAL—SHARKS, SQUID AND LAMPREY

The cartilaginous fishes (sharks, skates and rays) pose special problems for archaeologists because they have no bony skeleton, and few remains are therefore found in prehistoric sites. Some species have bony spines, but sometimes these are incorporated into portable artefacts, and therefore cannot be guaranteed to always end up on a midden. The skin of these fishes is covered with tiny denticles which are very durable and do survive, and there have been several attempts systematically to recover these (Fitch, 1967); however, there are great difficulties in working out MNI. Vertebrae sometimes survive in quite large numbers (Leach and Ward, 1981:58), and can be identified to species with X-rays (Desse and Desse, 1976), but the basic background research has yet to be completed in New Zealand. Any published MNI for these fish are very low minima.

Squid and octopus have a beak made of keratin-like protein and under some soil-chemical conditions these can survive in archaeological sites. Leach has identified one from the Fox River site, but this is exceptional. Low durability make it is unlikely that we will ever be able to obtain direct evidence of the relative importance of these animals in ancient diet.

The same type of problem prevails in the case of lamprey, and this is a great pity because there are good historic records that these fish were very important to some groups of Māori (Beattie, 1920:533ff, H.Leach, 1969:38). The chances of being able to assess the changing importance of this species archaeologically are very remote.

PREHISTORIC EXPLOITATION OF SEA MAMMALS

Although bones of sea mammals commonly occur in archaeological sites in New Zealand and the Chatham Islands, it is only recently that these have been studied in

Table 141: Total MNI of Fish for each Identification Taxon

Taxon Name	Family Name	MNI	%
Anguilla sp.	Anguillidae	64	0.52
Aplodactylus arctidens	Aplodactylidae	4	0.03
Arripis trutta	Arripidae	107	0.86
Caranx georgianus	Carangidae	18	0.15
Chelidonichthys kumu	Triglidae	39	0.31
Chrysophrys auratus	Sparidae	930	7.50
Conger sp.	Congridae	6	0.05
Conger verreauxi	Congridae	72	0.58
Elasmobranchii	Chondrichthyes	103	0.83
Genypterus blacodes	Ophidiidae	430	3.47
Kathetostoma giganteum	Uranoscopidae	4	0.03
Latridopsis ciliaris	Latrididae	59	0.48
Latris lineata	Latrididae	54	0.44
Leptoscopus macropygus	Leptoscopidae	8	0.06
Navodon convexirostris	Balistidae	72	0.58
Nemadactylus macropterus	Cheilodactylidae	324	2.61
Notothenia angustata	Nototheniidae	57	0.46
Odax pullus	Odacidae	62	0.50
Parapercis colias	Mugiloididae	729	5.88
Peltorhampus novaezeelandiae	Pleuronectidae	8	0.06
Polyprion oxygeneios	Percichthyidae	107	0.86
Pseudolabrus sp.	Labridae	1503	12.13
Pseudophycis bachus	Moridae	1234	9.96
Pseudophycis brevius	Moridae	1	0.01
Rexea solandri	Gempylidae	2	0.02
Rhombosolea sp.	Pleuronectidae	4	0.03
Scomber japonicus	Scombridae	1	0.01
Scorpaena cardinalis	Scorpaenidae	16	0.13
Scorpaenidae	Scorpaenidae	405	3.27
Seriola grandis	Carangidae	9	0.07
Seriolella brama	Centrolophidae	11	0.09
Teleostomi Species A	Osteichthyes	108	0.87
Teleostomi Species B	Osteichthyes	1	0.01
Thyrsites atun	Gempylidae	5795	46.76
Trachurus novaezelandiae	Carangidae	32	0.26
Zeus japonicus	Zeidae	14	0.11
Total		**12393**	

any detail by archaeologists. Almost all of the research in this field has been carried out by Dr Ian Smith of Otago University, in both the Chatham Islands (Smith 1976) and New Zealand (Smith 1985). The comments which follow are taken from Smith (1985:ii–iv). Smith has identified four principal methods of exploitation:

Scavenging from naturally stranded large cetaceans
Harpooning of smaller cetaceans
Occasional, opportunistic land-based seal hunting
Regular land-based seasonal cropping of seals.

Seal hunting took place predominantly during the late spring to early autumn, although in most regions of New Zealand there is some evidence of autumn-winter exploitation too. These pursuits made significant contributions to the diet of the Māori in pre-European times. Of interest is the lack of any archaeological evidence for ethno-historically documented seal hunting expeditions when large quantities of seal flesh were preserved. Smith documents both temporal and regional variations in sea mammal exploitation. It appears that in general these

Table 142: Total MNI of Fish for each Family

Family Name	Common Name	MNI	%
Chondrichthyes	Cartilaginous fishes	103	0.83
Osteichthyes	Bony fishes	109	0.88
Pleuronectidae	Right eyed flounders	12	0.10
Balistidae	Triggerfish	72	0.58
Anguillidae	Freshwater eels	64	0.52
Congridae	Conger eels	78	0.63
Ophidiidae	Cusk eels	430	3.47
Zeidae	Dories	14	0.11
Scombridae	Mackerel, Tuna	1	0.01
Gempylidae	Snake mackerels	5797	46.78
Uranoscopidae	Stargazers	4	0.03
Leptoscopidae	Stargazers	8	0.06
Centrolophidae	Raftfishes	11	0.09
Mugiloididae	Weevers	729	5.88
Nototheniidae	Ice Cods	57	0.46
Triglidae	Gurnards	39	0.31
Scorpaenidae	Scorpionfish	421	3.40
Carangidae	Jacks, Trevallies	59	0.48
Labridae	Wrasses	1503	12.13
Sparidae	Sea Breams	930	7.50
Cheilodactylidae	Morwongs	324	2.61
Aplodactylidae	Marblefishes	4	0.03
Percichthyidae	Basses	107	0.86
Arripidae	Kahawai	107	0.86
Latrididae	Trumpeters	113	0.91
Moridae	Morid cods	1235	9.97
Odacidae	Butterfishes	62	0.50
Total		**12393**	

a number of difficult assumptions in getting to this point, but the relative figures are very interesting (See Table 154). There is considerable regional and chronological variation, but in some cases this contribution is as high as 65%.

INSHORE AND OFFSHORE FISHING

Early Historical Evidence of Fishing Zones: Economic and Social Roles of Zones do not Coincide

The quality of information from early historic records varies greatly. From this distance in time it is now very difficult to be sure how to interpret accounts of behaviour which were relayed to interested third parties who wrote things down. It is a basic tenet in anthropological research that one cannot and should not interpret verbal accounts of behaviour literally and at face value. The social circumstances of 'question-and-answer' have a profound influence on what is said, and therefore what is recorded. The relationship between the two main parties is important, and also who else is listening to verbal exchange. Early European ethnographers were generally ignorant of these factors. One also has to remember that these records frequently have very little depth to them—in the case of fishing behaviour, early historic records from the Pacific generally tend to focus on the spectacular, the unusual, the things which were socially important. Thus, for the tropics there are numerous historic accounts of tuna fishing and practically no records at all of fishing for parrotfish. When reading these records, a century later, one might be forgiven for concluding that offshore fishing was far more important than fishing for humble fare in shallow waters; an anthropologist would not be forgiven for such an elementary error of scholarship.

Recorded eye witness accounts of offshore fishing can be very valuable, so long as we are careful to distinguish between the different social and economic roles. We also have to be careful in trying to interpret indirect evidence on this subject. A classic case is Marion du Fresne's observations of people in the Three Kings Islands:

pursuits were of greatest importance early in the prehistoric sequence, and persisted longest in southern parts of New Zealand. The timing and extent of the decline in importance of sea mammal hunting is quite variable. The changes in distribution and abundance of the main species appear to have been the direct result of human predation.

In Table 153 the MNI are given for sea mammals for all archaeological sites for which there is information. This is the basic information on which to base discussions about the relative importance these animals had in prehistoric diets, and how this changed in time and space. The large size of these animals compared with other flesh foods available to the Māori makes them especially important. Smith has calculated Meat Weights (MTWT) for sea mammals for the archaeological sites and has worked out the percent this contributed to the total meat in the diet. There are

"On the 10th we went in close and saw fires ashore; in closer still we saw men, which seemed to us most extraordinary in view of the apparent sterility of the country; they are probably inhabitants of the mainland who come to fish on these rocks" (Ollivier, 1985:125).

In many parts of the Pacific, skilled seafarers such as Polynesians make regular if infrequent trips to distant rocky outposts, like the Three Kings, precisely for fishing expeditions (and also birding). Only men go on these trips, and they live 'rough', and lie about telling stories late into the night. There is a clear parallel with modern trout fishing expeditions, although Europeans are less fussy about women taking part than most Polynesians. It is hard to judge the relative importance of recreational and economic roles of such trips, although in the case of modern trout fishing there is no doubt, since fish are frequently released after capture ! Did the Three Kings Islands function in this way for mainland Māori ? It may be difficult to answer this from archaeological evidence alone, because contrary to Marion du Fresne's conclusion it does appear that there was a permanent Māori population living there (Hayward, 1987:160). This does not rule out the possibility that these islands functioned as a fishing outpost too, but it does mean that it will be difficult to disentangle the two forms of evidence archaeologically.

In our opinion a close study of early historic records of the Māori could at best only reveal the social importance of offshore fishing. It is very unlikely that such a study would yield anything of value on the relative economic importance of inshore and offshore fishing.

Table 143: Total MNI for each Region using Identification Taxa

NNI = Northern North Island
SNI = Southern North Island
NSI = Northern South Island
SSI = Southern South Island
Chat = Chatham Islands

Taxon	NNI	SNI	NSI	SSI	Chat	Total
Anguilla sp.	3	29	-	1	31	64
Aplodactylus arctidens	-	3	-	1	-	4
Arripis trutta	27	78	2	-	0	107
Caranx georgianus	3	13	1	1	-	18
Chelidonichthys kumu	33	4	-	2	-	39
Chrysophrys auratus	488	269	163	10	-	930
Conger sp.	-	0	-	6	-	6
Conger verreauxi	-	22	4	37	9	72
Elasmobranchii	22	38	17	16	10	103
Genypterus blacodes	-	3	25	391	11	430
Kathetostoma giganteum	-	0	-	4	-	4
Latridopsis ciliaris	8	30	2	9	10	59
Latris lineata	-	1	-	52	1	54
Leptoscopus macropygus	-	0	-	0	8	8
Navodon convexirostris	63	-	2	7	-	72
Nemadactylus macropterus	19	16	5	191	93	324
Notothenia angustata	-	0	-	56	1	57
Odax pullus	-	38	-	19	5	62
Parapercis colias	10	13	5	614	87	729
Peltorhampus novaezeelandiae	-	0	1	7	-	8
Polyprion oxygeneios	2	10	16	74	5	107
Pseudolabrus sp.	34	129	11	1319	10	1503
Pseudophycis bachus	4	11	120	1099	-	1234
Pseudophycis brevius	-	0	-	1	-	1
Rexea solandri	-	1	-	1	-	2
Rhombosolea sp.	-	1	-	3	-	4
Scomber japonicus	-	1	-	0	-	1
Scorpaena cardinalis	-	4	-	12	-	16
Scorpaenidae	-	0	-	405	-	405
Seriola grandis	3	6	-	0	-	9
Seriolella brama	1	5	-	5	-	11
Teleostomi Species A	1	-	1	106	-	108
Teleostomi Species B	-	0	-	1	-	1
Thyrsites atun	21	57	340	5376	1	5795
Trachurus novaezelandiae	-	14	1	17	-	32
Zeus japonicus	3	11	-	0	-	14
Totals	**745**	**807**	**716**	**9843**	**282**	**12393**

Table 144: Fish % for each Region using Identification Taxa
These are worked out from the Total MNI for each region

NNI = Northern North Island
SNI = Southern North Island
NSI = Northern South Island
SSI = Southern South Island
Chat = Chatham Islands

Taxon	NNI	SNI	NSI	SSI	Chat
Anguilla sp.	0.40	3.59	-	0.01	10.99
Aplodactylus arctidens	-	0.37	-	0.01	-
Arripis trutta	3.62	9.67	0.28	-	-
Caranx georgianus	0.40	1.61	0.14	0.01	-
Chelidonichthys kumu	4.43	0.50	-	0.02	-
Chrysophrys auratus	65.50	33.33	22.77	0.10	-
Conger sp.	-	-	-	0.06	-
Conger verreauxi	-	2.73	0.56	0.38	3.19
Elasmobranchii	2.95	4.71	2.37	0.16	3.55
Genypterus blacodes	-	0.37	3.49	3.97	3.90
Kathetostoma giganteum	-	-	-	0.04	-
Latridopsis ciliaris	1.07	3.72	0.28	0.09	3.55
Latris lineata	-	0.12	-	0.53	0.35
Leptoscopus macropygus	-	-	-	-	2.84
Navodon convexirostris	8.46	-	0.28	0.07	-
Nemadactylus macropterus	2.55	1.98	0.70	1.94	32.98
Notothenia angustata	-	-	-	0.57	0.35
Odax pullus	-	4.71	-	0.19	1.77
Parapercis colias	1.34	1.61	0.70	6.24	30.85
Peltorhampus novaezeelandiae	-	-	0.14	0.07	-
Polyprion oxygeneios	0.27	1.24	2.23	0.75	1.77
Pseudolabrus sp.	4.56	15.99	1.54	13.40	3.55
Pseudophycis bachus	0.54	1.36	16.76	11.17	-
Pseudophycis brevius	-	-	-	0.01	-
Rexea solandri	-	0.12	-	0.01	-
Rhombosolea sp.	-	0.12	-	0.03	-
Scomber japonicus	-	0.12	-	-	-
Scorpaena cardinalis	-	0.50	-	0.12	-
Scorpaenidae	-	-	-	4.11	-
Seriola grandis	0.40	0.74	-	-	-
Seriolella brama	0.13	0.62	-	0.05	-
Teleostomi Species A	0.13	-	0.14	1.08	-
Teleostomi Species B	-	-	-	0.01	-
Thyrsites atun	2.82	7.06	47.49	54.62	0.35
Trachurus novaezelandiae	-	1.73	0.14	0.17	-
Zeus japonicus	0.40	1.36	-	-	-

Linguistic Evidence of Fishing Zones

There has recently been an attempt to use recorded Māori names for fishes as a guide to Māori knowledge of fish in different depth zones (Paulin 1989). This study assumes that "important aspects of early Maori life would be recorded in the language" (ibid.:2), but the author is perfectly well aware of the deficiencies of the information collected. In a 10 page paper there are no less than seven warnings that the lack of Māori names for many fishes was due to the ignorance of early

Europeans who were doing the recording. For example:

"The ignorance of the European in the ichthyofauna and the interest of historians only in large edible species are probably important reasons as to why so few Maori names have been preserved or why so many cannot be assigned to a species" (ibid.:5).

"The European settlers of New Zealand had little knowledge of the fishes present in New Zealand waters" (ibid.:5).

"Lack of European knowledge of the ichthyofauna also leave us in some doubt regarding the correct application of Maori names to particular fish species" (ibid.:5).

"If the Maori were acquainted with fishes found at depths of 50–100 m, the rarity of their occurrence was such that the Maori names were overlooked by the Europeans" (ibid.:8).

"Many species may have formed an important part of the Maori diet but because of cultural prejudices were not regarded as suitable food by Europeans and hence the recording of a name omitted because it was not regarded as necessary" (ibid.:10).

Table 145: Total MNI for each Region using Families

NNI = Northern North Island
SNI = Southern North Island
NSI = Northern South Island
SSI = Southern South Island
Chat = Chatham Islands

Family	NNI	SNI	NSI	SSI	Chat	Total
Chondrichthyes	22	38	17	16	10	103
Osteichthyes	1	-	1	107	-	109
Pleuronectidae	-	1	1	10	-	12
Balistidae	63	-	2	7	-	72
Anguillidae	3	29	-	1	31	64
Congridae	-	22	4	43	9	78
Ophidiidae	-	3	25	391	11	430
Zeidae	3	11	-	-	-	14
Scombridae	-	1	-	-	-	1
Gempylidae	21	58	340	5377	1	5797
Uranoscopidae	-	-	-	4	-	4
Leptoscopidae	-	-	-	-	8	8
Centrolophidae	1	5	-	5	-	11
Mugiloididae	10	13	5	614	87	729
Nototheniidae	-	-	-	56	1	57
Triglidae	33	4	-	2	-	39
Scorpaenidae	-	4	-	417	-	421
Carangidae	6	33	2	18	-	59
Labridae	34	129	11	1319	10	1503
Sparidae	488	269	163	10	-	930
Cheilodactylidae	19	16	5	191	93	324
Aplodactylidae	-	3	-	1	-	4
Percichthyidae	2	10	16	74	5	107
Arripidae	27	78	2	-	-	107
Latrididae	8	31	2	61	11	113
Moridae	4	11	120	1100	-	1235
Odacidae	-	38	-	19	5	62
Totals	**745**	**807**	**716**	**9843**	**282**	**12393**

In view of these problems it is hard to see how the author concludes that the Māori had "little apparent knowledge of fishes below 100 m depth" (ibid.:2). There could hardly be any Māori names recorded by Europeans for deep water fishes if the questioning Europeans themselves were ignorant of them. The study also concludes that the Māori had "a good knowledge...of oceanic or pelagic fish offshore" (ibid.).

There are several unsatisfactory things about trying to interpret historically recorded names like this. One of them is that the existence of a name for a species in a language does not necessarily imply that the species had any economic or social importance, but could mean merely that the people involved knew of the existence of the species. The assumption specified above that 'important aspects of early Maori life would be recorded in the language' does not necessarily work in the opposite direction—that is, a name does not mean it was important. Europeans have several names for seagulls, for example, yet they are not eaten by Europeans, nor do they have any special social significance to Europeans.

In short, knowledge of the resources of a fishing zone does not necessarily imply that these resources were harvested to any significant

Table 146: Fish % for each Region using Families
These are worked out from the Total MNI for each region

NNI = Northern North Island
SNI = Southern North Island
NSI = Northern South Island
SSI = Southern South Island
Chat = Chatham Islands

Family	NNI	SNI	NSI	SSI	Chat
Chondrichthyes	2.95	4.71	2.37	0.16	3.55
Osteichthyes	0.13	-	0.14	1.09	-
Pleuronectidae	-	0.12	0.14	0.10	-
Balistidae	8.46	-	0.28	0.07	-
Anguillidae	0.40	3.59	-	0.01	10.99
Congridae	-	2.73	0.56	0.44	3.19
Ophidiidae	-	0.37	3.49	3.97	3.90
Zeidae	0.40	1.36	-	-	-
Scombridae	-	0.12	-	-	-
Gempylidae	2.82	7.19	47.49	54.63	0.35
Uranoscopidae	-	-	-	0.04	-
Leptoscopidae	-	-	-	-	2.84
Centrolophidae	0.13	0.62	-	0.05	-
Mugiloididae	1.34	1.61	0.70	6.24	30.85
Nototheniidae	-	-	-	0.57	0.35
Triglidae	4.43	0.50	-	0.02	-
Scorpaenidae	-	0.50	-	4.24	-
Carangidae	0.81	4.09	0.28	0.18	-
Labridae	4.56	15.99	1.54	13.40	3.55
Sparidae	65.50	33.33	22.77	0.10	-
Cheilodactylidae	2.55	1.98	0.70	1.94	32.98
Aplodactylidae	-	0.37	-	0.01	-
Percichthyidae	0.27	1.24	2.23	0.75	1.77
Arripidae	3.62	9.67	0.28	-	-
Latrididae	1.07	3.84	0.28	0.62	3.90
Moridae	0.54	1.36	16.76	11.18	-
Odacidae	-	4.71	-	0.19	1.77

without a moment's thought that their method of classifying the natural environment is the only one with any useful meaning. When people from different cultural backgrounds come together and exchange names for fauna and flora they frequently 'talk past each other' because they have quite different taxonomies. There are several hints of this type of problem in the publication referred to (ibid.), for example in the discussion about the correct (meaning European) species which the names 'pakurakura' and 'maratea' refer to (ibid.:5). The common denominator for the four fish involved is a reddish colour, which incidentally is one of the simple meanings for the word 'pakurakura' (Tregear, 1891:309). The same type of problem could be suggested for the difficulty over the name 'tiitaki'.

One final point should be made about linguistic evidence on this subject—concerning the number of terms relating to particular species. Strickland (1989) notes that there are 14 Māori names for kahawai, 10 for yellow eyed mullet, and nine for snapper. This pales into insignificance, however, alongside 152 entries for terms of reference and varieties of eel in Strickland (1989:34–36). There is abundant anthropological literature relating linguistic complexity with social importance, and probably the best known example of this is the study by Evans-Prichard of the Nuer people who have literally several thousand expressions which refer to cattle (1940:45). On the strength of this, multiple names for eels, kahawai, yellow eyed mullet and snapper in Māori society should tell us something about the social importance of these species, and perhaps their economic value too. There is a wealth of direct evidence of this in the case of freshwater eels for the historic period (Marshall, 1987), but this example serves to highlight the dangers involved when trying to amalgamate historic and archaeological information. Bones of freshwater eels are very rare in New Zealand archaeological sites. It has been suggested that "eel head parts are small and fragile" (Sutton, 1986:310) and this is why

degree. The best way or working out ancient environmental knowledge and relative economic importance of different environments is to examine archaeological evidence. Yet this study reports that:

"archaeological evidence of fish species utilized by the Māori is incomplete and inconclusive" (Paulin, 1989:9).

We hope the present volume helps to rectify this problem.

Another important point which arises in a study like this concerns different kinds of taxonomy. Unfortunately many European scholars assume

Table 147: The 19 Numerically Important Fish Families by Region (%)

NNI = Northern North Island
SNI = Southern North Island
NSI = Northern South Island
SSI = Southern South Island
Chat = Chatham Islands

Family	NNI	SNI	NSI	SSI	Chat
Balistidae	8.46	-	0.28	0.07	-
Anguillidae	0.40	3.59	-	0.01	10.99
Congridae	-	2.73	0.56	0.44	3.19
Ophidiidae	-	0.37	3.49	3.97	3.90
Zeidae	0.40	1.36	-	-	-
Gempylidae	2.82	7.19	47.49	54.63	0.35
Leptoscopidae	-	-	-	-	2.84
Mugiloididae	1.34	1.61	0.70	6.24	30.85
Triglidae	4.43	0.50	-	0.02	-
Scorpaenidae	-	0.50	-	4.24	-
Carangidae	0.81	4.09	0.28	0.18	-
Labridae	4.56	15.99	1.54	13.40	3.55
Sparidae	65.50	33.33	22.77	0.10	-
Cheilodactylidae	2.55	1.98	0.70	1.94	32.98
Percichthyidae	0.27	1.24	2.23	0.75	1.77
Arripidae	3.62	9.67	0.28	-	-
Latrididae	1.07	3.84	0.28	0.62	3.90
Moridae	0.54	1.36	16.76	11.18	-
Odacidae	-	4.71	-	0.19	1.77

they are not found and identified by archaeologists. This is manifestly untrue because eel head bones occur in profusion in archaeological sites with a variety of soil chemical environments (Leach and Ward, 1981). This shows that this absence in old New Zealand sites is not due to preservation problems, but is far more likely to represent the loss of a food avoidance tapu relating to eels some time close to the first arrival of Europeans in New Zealand. The eel is a prime candidate for food avoidance in the Pacific and it has been shown that eels can occur in profusion and then disappear over archaeological time (Leach and Fleming *et al.* 1988) in response to changes in social attitude towards them.

What this example shows is that archaeological and historic information about human behaviour cannot always be simply added together to produce a richer picture of past human society. They do not always just add together. The apparent discrepancy with eels, in our view, re-affirms that there were significant changes taking place in Māori society early in the protohistoric period. In this regard it is useful to be able to point to considerable direct archaeological evidence for eels at the Parewanui site in Manawatu (see Appendix Tables 117–118, and Cassels *et al.*, 1988), dated to the nineteenth century.

Paulin concludes that "the pre-European Maori of New Zealand had...little knowledge of fishes from below depths of 100 m" (ibid.:2). In our view this conclusion cannot be reached on the basis of the type of information presented. He comments further "The great abundance of fishes around New Zealand...made it unnecessary for the Maori to venture beyond the immediate coastline: indeed Heaphy ...remarked on the absence of any ocean-going canoes at one community on the west coast of the South island" (ibid.:9). The first comment does not show much understanding of why Polynesians put to sea in open craft, because it is seldom a matter of necessity and more often for adventure and interesting fishing. As for the west coast group referred to, these people had an unusual economy with strong seasonal specializations. It has been studied in depth by H. Leach (1969), and the lack of ocean-going canoes is not out of character when a more detailed picture of the culture is considered (ibid.:67).

The Archaeological Evidence of Fishing Zones

There is abundant evidence in the New Zealand archaeological record that the Māori people spent a significant amount of their time exploiting the inshore marine environment. It is much less clear how much time they spent at significant distances (more than say 5 km) offshore. The lack of direct

Table 148: MNI by Periods for Identification Taxa
Number of assemblages = 1000
1 = Archaic New Zealand Polynesian
2 = Classic Māori
3 = Post-European

Taxon	1	2	3	Total
Anguilla sp.	1	34	29	64
Aplodactylus arctidens	-	3	1	4
Arripis trutta	74	27	6	107
Caranx georgianus	8	6	4	18
Chelidonichthys kumu	6	31	2	39
Chrysophrys auratus	563	342	25	930
Conger sp.	3	1	2	6
Conger verreauxi	16	38	18	72
Elasmobranchii	19	65	19	103
Genypterus blacodes	265	130	35	430
Kathetostoma giganteum	-	1	3	4
Latridopsis ciliaris	6	43	10	59
Latris lineata	16	16	22	54
Leptoscopus macropygus	-	8	-	8
Navodon convexirostris	17	50	5	72
Nemadactylus macropterus	33	175	116	324
Notothenia angustata	49	5	3	57
Odax pullus	6	44	12	62
Parapercis colias	205	272	252	729
Peltorhampus novaezeelandiae	7	1	-	8
Polyprion oxygeneios	23	83	1	107
Pseudolabrus sp.	337	375	791	1503
Pseudophycis bachus	763	386	85	1234
Pseudophycis brevius	-	1	-	1
Rexea solandri	-	1	1	2
Rhombosolea sp.	-	3	1	4
Scomber japonicus	-	1	-	1
Scorpaena cardinalis	-	9	7	16
Scorpaenidae	52	180	173	405
Seriola grandis	-	9	-	9
Seriolella brama	1	6	4	11
Teleostomi Species A	73	33	2	108
Teleostomi Species B	1	-	-	1
Thyrsites atun	4233	1420	142	5795
Trachurus novaezelandiae	1	25	6	32
Zeus japonicus	2	7	5	14
Totals	**6780**	**3831**	**1782**	**12393**

It is important to realise that there are basically two kinds of fish in offshore waters—those which have to be caught with long lines in very deep waters, and those which are taken on the surface, usually with trolling lures. There is very little ethnographic evidence from anywhere in the Pacific that Austronesian people fished in very deep water offshore, though there is a great deal about fishing in the surface of offshore waters. The significant exception to this is fishing for 'palu', the Ruvettus or oil fish. A distinctive wooden hook is often interpreted by ethnologists as evidence of palu fishing in different islands, and this hook is known from New Zealand (Burrows, 1938:11; Fairfield, 1933). Not one bone of this fish has been found so far in any Pacific excavation, including New Zealand. There are two possible reasons for this: either the bones have been mistaken for another species or this specialized fishing spread rapidly in the early European era, and middens belonging to this period have not been investigated thoroughly. Neither of these alternatives can be ruled out at the moment.

evidence on this point does not necessarily mean a lack of activity in this zone. Historic studies of Pacific island fishermen and comparison with archaeological evidence has shown that the offshore waters can be extremely important to a group of fishermen, but that relatively few fish may be caught there and end up in midden sites on the land (Leach and Davidson, 1988).

However, since we are personally responsible for a large number of the identifications of allied species we should make a comment about the first option. It was only after some difficulty that we managed to get a single specimen of the palu species recently, and the cranial anatomy is very similar to several oceanic pelagic fish, and could easily have been mistaken for them in the past.

These include barracouta, the southem kingfish, the frostfish, and members of the tuna group (see Table 155). It will be necessary to re-examine all archaeological bones from these species to check their identifications in the future. It is unlikely that many of the bones identified in the past as barracouta are actually palu, but some of them may be.

Assuming that these difficult identifications are confirmed, what does the accumulated bone evidence tell us ? With the exception of a few species, most fishes caught by the pre-European Māori are most easily taken by inshore fishing, using nets and baited hooks. The possible exceptions to this are given in Table 156. These fish can be caught at considerable distances offshore, but they can also be taken in shallow waters, such as harbours during seasonal movements. At the present time there is no reliable method for deciding where they were caught.

One other area of archaeological evidence should be mentioned. This concems the movement of raw materials from one place to another. The prehistoric Māori had an elaborate trading system throughout New Zealand, and archaeologists have investigated this by tracing the movement of durable raw materials like obsidian and other stones, using trace element fingerprinting techniques (Leach and Manly, 1982). These studies have also revealed that the prehistoric Māori visited the Chatham islands and the Kermadecs (Leach and Anderson *et al.*, 1986). Whether this contact was the result of regular two-way navigated voyages can be debated, but it certainly shows that the Māori were no strangers to the open sea.

Conclusion

In our opinion, historic evidence relating to fishing in the offshore zone is seldom very helpful in shedding light on the economic importance of this area, but it is frequently a good guide to its social importance.

Table 149: Percentage Values by Periods for Identification Taxa
These are worked out from the Total MNI for each Period. Number of assemblages = 1000
1 = Archaic New Zealand Polynesian
2 = Classic Māori
3 = Post-European

Taxon	1	2	3
Anguilla sp.	0.01	0.89	1.63
Aplodactylus arctidens	-	0.08	0.06
Arripis trutta	1.09	0.70	0.34
Caranx georgianus	0.12	0.16	0.22
Chelidonichthys kumu	0.09	0.81	0.11
Chrysophrys auratus	8.30	8.93	1.40
Conger sp.	0.04	0.03	0.11
Conger verreauxi	0.24	0.99	1.01
Elasmobranchii	0.28	1.70	1.07
Genypterus blacodes	3.91	3.39	1.96
Kathetostoma giganteum	-	0.03	0.17
Latridopsis ciliaris	0.09	1.12	0.56
Latris lineata	0.24	0.42	1.23
Leptoscopus macropygus	-	0.21	-
Navodon convexirostris	0.25	1.31	0.28
Nemadactylus macropterus	0.49	4.57	6.51
Notothenia angustata	0.72	0.13	0.17
Odax pullus	0.09	1.15	0.67
Parapercis colias	3.02	7.10	14.14
Peltorhampus novaezeelandiae	0.10	0.03	-
Polyprion oxygeneios	0.34	2.17	0.06
Pseudolabrus sp.	4.97	9.79	44.39
Pseudophycis bachus	11.25	10.08	4.77
Pseudophycis brevius	-	0.03	-
Rexea solandri	-	0.03	0.06
Rhombosolea sp.	-	0.08	0.06
Scomber japonicus	-	0.03	-
Scorpaena cardinalis	-	0.23	0.39
Scorpaenidae	0.77	4.70	9.71
Seriola grandis	-	0.23	-
Seriolella brama	0.01	0.16	0.22
Teleostomi Species A	1.08	0.86	0.11
Teleostomi Species B	0.01	-	-
Thyrsites atun	62.43	37.07	7.97
Trachurus novaezelandiae	0.01	0.65	0.34
Zeus japonicus	0.03	0.18	0.28

We also think the conclusion that 'the Māori had little knowledge of fish below 100m' on the grounds of linguistic evidence, is based on misinterpretations because, on the one hand, there has been a failure to take adequate notice of the extent of ignorance of early Europeans about New Zealand fish species, and on the other, there was a conflict between two folk taxonomies, and the parties involved did not understand each other properly when the linguistic data were recorded.

There is abundant direct archaeological evidence that the pre-European Māori obtained large numbers of fish from the inshore environment, but very little direct and unambiguous evidence that either deep water or offshore species were economically significant. On the other hand, other forms of direct evidence, such as the transport of New Zealand obsidian to both the Chatham Islands and the Kermadecs, certainly show that the pre-European Māori were venturing away from coastal waters.

MARINE RESOURCE MANAGEMENT

Romantic writers of the 19th century frequently characterized Polynesian people and other small-scale societies as having an idyllic life as 'noble savages in harmony with nature'. Early anthropologists quickly dispelled this notion. In 1950, Piddington remarked:

"Thus we have disposed of the 'noble savage', that amiable imbecile who meanders through the ethnological writings of Elliot Smith. We have seen that primitive man is upon occasion aggressive, greedy and even disloyal to the cultural standards by which he lives. We have seen that his economic life is dominated not by a 'communist group sentiment', but by a complex of motives in which self-interest, personal sentiment, respect for tradition and fear of supernatural sanctions are

inextricably interwoven" (Piddington, 1952:393).

Life in prehistoric New Zealand was anything but idyllic, and the idea that the Māori people were living in harmony with nature is naive. Many people are surprised to learn that the average age at death for New Zealand as a whole for the prehistoric period was only 31 or 32 years of age (Houghton, 1980:97). Detailed studies of prehistoric communities and their relationship with the environment in the Palliser Bay region revealed a complex history of declining economic resources until people were forced to abandon the region (Leach and Leach, 1979). Although the basic theme in this reconstruction is now widely accepted, many people still cling to the more idyllic view, and pass off the Palliser Bay

Table 150: MNI by Periods for Families
1 = Archaic New Zealand Polynesian
2 = Classic Māori
3 = Post-European

Family	1	2	3	Total
Chondrichthyes	19	65	19	103
Osteichthyes	74	33	2	109
Pleuronectidae	7	4	1	12
Balistidae	17	50	5	72
Anguillidae	1	34	29	64
Congridae	19	39	20	78
Ophidiidae	265	130	35	430
Zeidae	2	7	5	14
Scombridae	-	1	-	1
Gempylidae	4233	1421	143	5797
Uranoscopidae	-	1	3	4
Leptoscopidae	-	8	-	8
Centrolophidae	1	6	4	11
Mugiloididae	205	272	252	729
Nototheniidae	49	5	3	57
Triglidae	6	31	2	39
Scorpaenidae	52	189	180	421
Carangidae	9	40	10	59
Labridae	337	375	791	1503
Sparidae	563	342	25	930
Cheilodactylidae	33	175	116	324
Aplodactylidae	-	3	1	4
Percichthyidae	23	83	1	107
Arripidae	74	27	6	107
Latrididae	22	59	32	113
Moridae	763	387	85	1235
Odacidae	6	44	12	62
Totals	**6780**	**3831**	**1782**	**12393**

Table 151: Percentage Values by Periods for Families
These are worked out from the Total MNI for each Period
1 = Archaic New Zealand Polynesian
2 = Classic Māori
3 = Post-European

Family	1	2	3
Chondrichthyes	0.28	1.70	1.07
Osteichthyes	1.09	0.86	0.11
Pleuronectidae	0.10	0.10	0.06
Balistidae	0.25	1.31	0.28
Anguillidae	0.01	0.89	1.63
Congridae	0.28	1.02	1.12
Ophidiidae	3.91	3.39	1.96
Zeidae	0.03	0.18	0.28
Scombridae	-	0.03	-
Gempylidae	62.43	37.09	8.02
Uranoscopidae	-	0.03	0.17
Leptoscopidae	-	0.21	-
Centrolophidae	0.01	0.16	0.22
Mugiloididae	3.02	7.10	14.14
Nototheniidae	0.72	0.13	0.17
Triglidae	0.09	0.81	0.11
Scorpaenidae	0.77	4.93	10.10
Carangidae	0.13	1.04	0.56
Labridae	4.97	9.79	44.39
Sparidae	8.30	8.93	1.40
Cheilodactylidae	0.49	4.57	6.51
Aplodactylidae	-	0.08	0.06
Percichthyidae	0.34	2.17	0.06
Arripidae	1.09	0.70	0.34
Latrididae	0.32	1.54	1.80
Moridae	11.25	10.10	4.77
Odacidae	0.09	1.15	0.67

Table 152: MNI of Crayfish in New Zealand and Chatham Islands
After Leach and Anderson (1979:152). Waihora figures after Sutton (1979:136).

Site Name	Site No	MNI
Black Rocks BR4	N168/77	947
Black Rocks BR3	N168/77	481
Black Rocks BR2	N168/77	101
Washpool Midden	N168/22	3
CHB	C240/680	31
Waihora	C240/283	11
Te Ngaio	C240/277	3

evidence as an unusual case of prehistoric environmental mis-management. Few archaeologists would agree with this.

In the case of fishing behaviour there is support in some quarters for the view that "traditional knowledge can be invaluable to Western scientists as an aid in conserving natural resources" (Johannes, 1981:148). Detailed studies along these lines have been made by Johannes for the Belau people in the northwest Pacific. What his study fails to take into account, however, is the disjunction between ideal and actual behaviour noted earlier. Since Johannes' work in Belau there has been a detailed study of the prehistory of fishing in this island group and this throws into sharp relief the difference between what fishermen say they do and what they really did in practice over some 3000 years (Fleming, 1986).

There is now considerable interest in gathering scholarly information on the environmental effects of human predation, but for marine resources this work is in its infancy. In addition to changes in natural distribution and relative abundance which can be documented by normal archaeological techniques, metrical data on population characteristics is slowly being won from the soil. This is a very large undertaking, because live animal characteristics need to be reconstructed from bone fragments. This needs large statistical samples of bones from modern specimens, and measurements on archaeological bones. Work on this has now started in New Zealand (Boocock, 1986).

It is also desirable to consider more than one theoretical model of the way in which ancient people might have thought about resource management and therefore regulated their behaviour with rules or customs. It is customary to think in quite simple terms about this—'only take specimens of a certain size and number so as not to adversely affect the natural population'. This might be called a 'constant feedback' model, and may be quite inappropriate to prehistoric communities, who had such a different settlement pattern to modern communities. It has been shown by H.Leach (1969) that South Island communities in particular were very mobile and chased seasonally rich resources. Their attitude and actual behaviour towards harvesting marine resources may have been very different to the 'constant feedback' model.

An alternative model which is worth considering for some communities involves intensive use of a resource followed by a fallow period for it to recover. Māori horticulture has often been referred to as 'slash and bum and fallow' in approach. This same concept could have applied to marine resources too. The concept has a respectable ancestry of several thousand years for Austronesian communities, of which tropical Polynesians and the Māori are descendants. In New Britain, for example, the inland people clear land of forest, intensively garden, and then leave it to fallow for many years. A very similar pattem has been reconstructed by H.Leach for the Palliser Bay people (H.Leach, 1976).

Information bearing on this issue for marine food gathering is hard to find at the moment, because the basic background research has yet to be done. What can be said at the moment is that wherever there have been detailed archaeological studies on this subject in New Zealand, marine resources can be seen to decline in mean size over time, and species can be shown to disappear. Cases of this which can be cited are: dramatic lowering of mean size of crayfish and paua at Palliser Bay (Leach and Anderson, 1979), loss of shellfish species in Palliser Bay (Leach and Leach, 1979), changes in the natural distribution of sea mammals in New Zealand (Smith, 1985).

In short, it is hard to make a convincing case that the prehistoric Māori were skilled in marine resource management.

Table 153: Minimum Numbers of Individuals (MNI) of Sea Mammals Page references are to Smith (1985) with the exception of site CHC, which refers to Smith (1976), and of Waihora, which refers to Sutton (1979).

A = New Zealand fur seal, *Arctocephalus forsteri*
B = New Zealand sea lion, *Phocarctus hookeri*
C = Southem elephant seal, *Mirounga leonina*
D = Leopard seal, *Hydrurga leptonyx*
E = Cetaceans, largely the following species: Pilot whales, *Globicephala malaena*, *G. macrorhynchus*. Dolphins, *Delphinus delphis*, *Lagenorhynchus obscurus*

Site Name	Site No	Ref	A	B	C	D	E
Houhora	N6/4	p.282	44	8	7	-	2
Smugglers Cove	N24/13	p.277	1	-	-	-	1
Sunde Site	N38/24	p.273	2	1	-	-	-
Parker's Midden	N40/2	p.257	1	1	-	-	1.
Opito Beach	N40/3	p.260	17	-	2	-	3
Sarah's Gully	N40/9	p.267	4	-	1	-	8
Tairua	N44/2	p.239	9	1	1	-	1
Hot Water Beach	N44/69	p.249 ff	5	-	-	-	-
Whangamata Wharf	N49/2	p.512	2	-	-	-	-
Kaupokonui	N128/3B	p.233	-	15	1	-	-
Paremata	N160/50	p.228	19	8	4	-	4
Washpool Midden	N168-9/22	p.214	2	2	2	-	3
Black Rocks	N168-9/77	p.221	5	-	-	-	2
Rotokura	S14/1	p.203	18	10	5	1	1
Huriawa Pa	S155/1	p.510	1	-	-	-	-
Pleasant River A	S155/2	p.511	5	3	6	-	-
Pleasant River 2	S155/8	p.197	3	-	1	1	1
Ross's Rocks	S155/38	p.194	5	-	-	-	2
Papanui	S164/1	p.176	17	2	-	-	-
Mapoutahi	S164/13	p.509	1	-	-	-	-
Purakanui	S164/18	p.190	2	-	-	-	-
Long Beach	S164/20	p.184	7	2	2	1	2
Taiaroa Head	S164/191	p.508	1	-	-	-	-
Riverton	S176/1	p.148	2	3	-	-	1
Wakapatu	S176/4	p.152	3	-	-	-	1
Tiwai Point	S181-2/16	p.136	21	5	6	-	-
Pounawea	S184/1	p.169	13	9	3	-	-
Papatowai Point	S184/5	p.156	10	4	1	1	-
West Point	S187/4	p.506	2	1	-	-	-
Parangiaio Point	S187/9	p.507	5	2	-	-	-
Lee Island	S187/11	p.505	11	1	-	-	-
CHC	C240/689	p.39,65	130	2	12	8	-
Waihora	C240/283	p.133,151	31	1	-	-	-

THE EXTENT OF RELIANCE ON MARINE RESOURCES—ISOTOPE RESEARCH

Another important area of research which bears on early fishing activities concerns trace element and isotope levels in prehistoric populations. Research in this area is only just beginning in New Zealand, but has already provided important information about early diet in the Pacific region (Horwood, 1989; Leach *et al.*, n.d.). This new archaeological technique requires analysis of a fragment of human bone and enables us to calculate the percentage of total food intake which comes from the land or sea, and information on some further zones and food components within these two main categories. This work has shown that the Moriori people of the Chatham Islands received about 90% of their total food energy from marine resources from determination of levels of ^{15}N, ^{13}C, and ^{34}S isotopes in bone samples. This high proportion of marine food in the diet is amongst the highest values known anywhere in the world.

This important new avenue of research will, in due course, provide quantitative information on the dietary importance of marine foods for coastal and inland Māori groups in New Zealand at different time periods.

Table 154: Percent Total MTWT from Seals in Diet
This information is taken from Smith (1986:337-8).

A = Northern North island
B = Palliser Bay
C = East Otago
D = Catlins
E = Foveaux Strait

Period	A	B	C	D	E
18th Century	-	7	11	-	-
17th Century	-	-	-	-	55
16th Century	-	-	45	-	-
14th Century	40	-	27	27	50
13-14th Century	-	16	-	-	-
12th Century	-	12	-	65	-

SUMMARY AND CONCLUDING COMMENTS

The main objective of this volume was to put together as much reliable data as possible on fish catches of the pre-European Māori people. Methods of analysis of faunal material have not been standardized in the past, so we have primarily relied on data which we have been personally responsible for. In addition to this, summaries are provided of data from published literature in cases where we consider the results are reasonably compatible with our own. However, for the purposes of broad characterizations of fish catches in time and space we have not used these additional data.

In several places in this volume we have warned that for the protohistoric period in New Zealand it is not possible simply to add together ethnohistoric and archaeological data. This is a very special period of rapid cultural change in the Pacific region generally, and specialized skills are required in correctly interpreting these two lines of evidence in the same context. There are few scholars who are expert in this task in New Zealand. In the area of fishing behaviour in particular there are additional problems—fishing is one aspect of behaviour in which people have good reason to be vague about their knowledge, make exaggerated claims about their catches or false reports of where they were caught, and at times fishermen manage to fool themselves about these things too. There is no reason to think that the New Zealand case should be any different to elsewhere in the

Table 155: Offshore and Inshore species with Similar Anatomy
The cranial anatomy of the following species are difficult to distinguish, especially with bone fragments. The MNI given are totals for New Zealand from Appendix 8.

Species	Common Name	Family	MNI
Thyrsites atun	Barracouta	Gempylidae	5795
Rexea solandri	Southern Kingfish	Gempylidae	2
Ruvettus pretiosus	Oilfish	Gempylidae	0
Lepidopus caudatus	Frostfish	Trichiuridae	0
Katsuwonis pelamis, etc.	Skipjack tuna, etc.	Scombridae	0

Pacific. The best evidence about what people were actually catching is found in archaeological sites. However, ethnohistoric evidence is very valuable in defining the social importance of different marine resources. The two lines of evidence therefore are complementary in the sense that they usually describe different aspects of society.

One area in which this is especially relevant concerns the role of offshore fishing. Studies of Pacific fishing lead us to believe that the offshore zone is of very great importance to many Polynesian fishermen, not economically but socially. The role of the inshore zone is the exact opposite—it is of great economic importance but has far less social significance. In some societies this distinction between offshore and inshore is correlated with the difference between men and women because, although women are permitted to forage for food in the shallow waters of reef flats, only men may venture to sea for adventurous fishing expeditions. Archaeological evidence from many places in the Pacific supports the view that far more food was collected close to shore than in the open sea. Unfortunately, it is probably too late to document these distinctions as thoroughly in New Zealand as in the Pacific, but we believe they are just as applicable here.

The best evidence which bears on the question 'how important were marine foods to the Māori' comes from isotope and trace element studies, not from midden analysis. Unfortunately results in this area are incomplete—however we do have reliable results for the Chathams islands and these indicate that about 90% of all food energy consumed by these people came from the sea. Such a high figure is comparable to the Alaskan Eskimo (see also Sutton 1989:127). Figures for the mainland New Zealand Māori are unlikely to be quite as high as this, but archaeological evidence from sea mammal exploitation alone shows that the sea was very important in the overall diet. Just how important requires further research with isotopes.

On the subject of resource management, there is a problem of perception here—most commentators on this subject take an unduly

Table 156: Predatory Pelagic Fish Probably Caught with Lures		
Family	Common Name	MNI
Gempylidae	Snake mackerels	5797
Arripidae	Kahawai	107
Carangidae	Jacks, Trevallies	59
Scombridae	Mackerel, Tuna	1

simplistic position that conserving the environment means making only modest demands on resources on a fairly constant basis. This position presupposes a modem form of settlement pattem where people stay in one place for long periods. However, many prehistoric communities were not like this at all, but had both central place and satellite settlements to take advantage of seasonally abundant resources, and many of those who engaged in horticulture would have shifted these settlement components over longer periods to allow land to fallow. The basic horticultural model which was followed in New Zealand is known as 'slash and bum and fallow', and this has great antiquity in the Pacific. This is devastating on local resources in the short term, but the fallow period allows eventual recovery. This type of. resource management policy can also be seen as conservationist in approach, but a longer period of reference needs to be considered. It is quite possible that marine resource management policies were similar in structure to this in some cases. Whether this model is more appropriate than the 'modest exploitation' one or not, there is overwhelming archaeological evidence that marine resources were adversely affected by Māori occupation over the last thousand years. It has been shown that some breeding colonies of sea mammals disappeared, and the overall distribution of some species was affected by human predation. It has also been shown that shellfish species and crayfish dramatically decreased in mean size in some regions with sustained harvesting. Land based changes, brought about by deforestation, in some areas wiped out some marine species altogether from the increased sediment loads in rivers being dumped into the sea. As far as bony fish are concemed, at the moment we know very little about either the short term or long term effects of human predation in New Zealand. This requires gathering evidence about the original live fish sizes by mathematical reconstruction from archaeological bones. Research of this kind has only recently been started in Pacific Island archaeology, and much background research is still needed in New Zealand.

The general character of fish bones in archaeological sites clearly shows that far more inshore species (and specimens of them) were caught than deep water or offshore ones. It was pointed out that archaeological indicators of offshore fishing are ambiguous, because the main targets are likely to have been pelagic rather than demersal species, and these can also be taken inshore. Thus, present evidence for offshore fishing could be substantially under-estimated. In the future, isotope evidence may help to document this better.

There are substantial differences in the character of fish catches from one region to another, and these partly reflect changes in natural abundance. There are also indications of significant changes over time, but this is complicated by uneven knowledge of communities at different periods in New Zealand.

REFERENCES CITED

Allingham,B. 1988a. Personal communication. C/O Post Office, Waikouaiti, Otago.

Allingham,B. 1988b. Preliminary report on salvage excavations at Tumbledown Bay, Banks Peninsula. Unpublished report under Permit 1987/9, New Zealand Historic Places Trust.

Allo,J. 1972. The Whangamata Wharf site (N49/2): excavations on a Coromandel coastal midden. *Records of the Auckland Institute and Museum* 9:61–79.

Anderson,A.J. 1979. Excavations at the Archaic site of Waianakarua Mouth, North Otago. *New Zealand Archaeological Association Newsletter* 22(4):156–161.

Anderson,A.J. 1981. A fourteenth-century fishing camp at Purakanui Inlet, Otago. *Journal of the Royal Society of New Zealand* 11(3):201–221.

Anderson,A.J. 1981. Barracouta fishing in prehistoric and early historic New Zealand. *Journal de la Société des Océanistes* 34(72–73):145–158.

Anderson,A.J. 1982. The Otakia Mouth site at Brighton Beach, Otago. *New Zealand Archaeological Association Newsletter* 25(1):47–52.

Anderson,A.J. 1982. West Coast, South Island. *In* N.Prickett (ed.), *The first thousand years: regional perspectives in New Zealand archaeology*. New Zealand Archaeological Association Monograph 13, Dunmore Press, Palmerston North:103–11.

Anderson,A.J. 1983. Analysis of fish remains from Southern Fiordland and Stewart Island. *New Zealand Archaeological Association Newsletter* 26(4):264–268.

Beattie,H. 1920. Nature-lore of the southern Maori. *Transactions of the New Zealand Institute* LII:53–77.

Bellwood,P. 1978. *Man's conquest of the Pacific.* William Collins Publishers Ltd, Auckland.

Boocock,A.S. 1986. A method for the reconstruction of the live weight and length of snapper *(Chrysophrys auratus* [Forster]) from archaeological bones. Unpublished BA Hons dissertation, Anthropology, University of Otago.

Boocock,A.S. 1990. Fishing in early New Zealand: a study of archaeological fishbones. Unpublished MA thesis, Anthropology, University of Otago.

Brailsford,B. 1981. *The tattooed land: the southern frontiers of the pa Maori.* A.H. & A.W. Reed, Wellington.

Brailsford,B. 1984. *Greenstone trails: the Maori search for Pounamu.* A.H. & A.W. Reed, Wellington.

Burrows,E.G. 1938. *Western Polynesia: a study in cultural differentiation.* Etnologiska Studier (Göteborg) 7.

Butts,D.J. 1977. Seasonality at Rotokura, Tasman Bay: a case study in the use of faunal identifications to establish the season of occupation for an archaeological site. Unpublished BA(Hons) dissertation, Anthropology, University of Otago.

Cannon,D.Y. 1987. *Marine fish osteology: A manual for archaeologists.* Department of Archaeology, Simon Fraser University.

Cassels,R.J.S., Jones,K.L., Walton,A. and Worthy,T.H. 1988. Late prehistoric subsistence practices at Parewanui, lower Rangitikei River, New Zealand. *New Zealand Journal of Archaeology* 10:109–128.

Casteel,R.W. 1976. *Fish remains in archaeology and palaeoènvironmental studies.* Academic Press.

Courtemanche,M. and Legrendre,V. 1985. *Os de poissons: Nomenclature codifiée noms Français et Anglais.* UQAM, Département des Sciences de la Terre, Montreal.

Coutts,P.J.F. 1969. Archaeology in Fiordland, New Zealand. *New Zealand Archaeological Association Newsletter* 12(3):117–123.

Coutts,P.J.F. 1970. The Port Craig—Sandhill Point regions of Southland: a preliminary archaeological report. *Archaeology and Physical Anthropology in Oceania* 5(1):53–59.

Coutts,P.J.F. 1971a. Archaeological studies at Martin's Bay. *Journal of the Polynesian Society* 80(2):170–203.

Coutts,P.J.F. 1971b. Greenstone: the prehistoric exploitation of bowenite from Anita bay, Milford Sound. *Journal of the Polynesian Society* 80(1):42–73.

Coutts,P.J.F. 1972. The emergence of the Foveaux Strait Maori from prehistory: a study of culture contact. Unpublished PhD dissertation, Anthropology, University of Otago.

Coutts,P.J.F. 1975. Marine fishing in archaeological perspective: techniques for determining fishing strategies. *In* R.W.Casteel and G.I.Quimby (eds), *Maritime Adaptations of the Pacific*: 265–306. World Anthropology, Mouton Publishers, The Hague, Paris.

Coutts,P.J.F. 1977. Archaeological studies in Dusky and Breaksea Sounds, southwestern Fiordland, New Zealand: a summary. *Journal of the Polynesian Society* 86(1):37–72.

Coutts,P.J.F. and Jurisich,M. 1972. *Results of an archaeological survey of Ruapuke Island.* Otago University Monographs in Prehistoric Anthropology 5.

Davidson,J.M. 1970. Excavation of an "undefended" site, N38/37, on Motutapu Island, New Zealand. *Records of the Auckland Institute and Museum* 7:31–60.

Davidson,J.M. 1972. Archaeological investigations on Motutapu Island, New Zealand: an introduction to recent fieldwork and some further results. *Records of the Auckland Institute and Museum* 9:1–14.

Davidson,J.M. 1976. Survey and excavations at Te Ika-a-maru Bay, Wellington, 1962–63. *New Zealand Archaeological Association Newsletter* 19(1):4–25.

Davidson,J.M. 1978. Archaeological salvage excavations at Paremata, Wellington, New Zealand. *National Museum of New Zealand Records* 1(13):203–236.

Davidson,J.M. 1979. Archaic middens of the Coromandel region: a review. *In* A.Anderson (ed.), *Birds of a feather.* New Zealand Archaeological Association Monograph 11, BAR International Series S62:183–202.

Davidson,J.M. 1982. Auckland. *In* N.Prickett (ed.), *The first thousand years: regional perspectives in New Zealand archaeology.* New Zealand Archaeological Association Monograph 13, Dunmore Press, Palmerston North.

Davidson,J.M. 1984. *The prehistory of New Zealand.* Longman Paul Ltd, Auckland.

Davidson,J.M. 1988. Personal Communication. National Museum of New Zealand, Wellington.

Desse,G. and Desse,J. 1976. *Diagnostic des pièces rachidiennes des Téléostéens et des Chondrichthyens.* Expansion Scientifique.

Desse-Berset,N. 1984. *2ièmes Rencontres d'archéo-ichthyologie.* CNRS Notes et Monographies Techniques № 16.

Evans-Pritchard,E.E. 1940. *The Nuer.* Clarendon Press, Oxford.

Fairfield,F.G. 1933. Maori fish-hooks from Manukau Heads, Auckland. *Journal of the Polynesian Society* 42:145–155.

Fitch,J.E. 1967. Fish remains recovered from a Corona del Mar, California, Indian midden (ORA–190). *California Fish and Game* 53(3):195–191.

Fleming,M.A. 1986. The scaridae family in Pacific prehistory. Unpublished MA thesis, Anthropology, University of Otago.

Furey,L. 1982. A review of Coromandel Peninsula excavation literature. *New Zealand Archaeological Association Newsletter* 25(1):30–46.

Fyfe,R. 1982. The fishing behaviour of the prehistoric inhabitants of Long Beach, Otago. Unpublished MA thesis, Anthropology, University of Otago.

Hamel,G.E and Leach,H.M. 1979. Radiocarbon dates from Long Beach, Otago, New Zealand. *New Zealand Archaeological Association Newsletter* 22(3):128.

Hamel,G.E. 1977. Prehistoric man and his environment in the Catlins, New Zealand. Unpublished PhD dissertation, Anthropology, University of Otago.

Hayward,B.W. 1987. Prehistoric archaeological sites on the Three Kings Islands, Northern New Zealand. *Records of the Auckland Institute and Museum* 24:147–161.

Heaphy,C. 1846. Notes of an expedition to Kawatiri and Araura, on the western coast of the middle island. In N.M.Taylor (ed.), 1959. *Early travellers in New Zealand*: 203–249. Clarendon Press, Oxford.

Higham,C.F.W. 1968. Prehistoric research in western Southland. *New Zealand Archaeological Association Newsletter* 11(4):155–164.

Higham,C.F.W. 1970. The role of economic prehistory in the interpretation of settlement of Oceania. In Green,R.C. and Kelly,M. (eds), *Studies in Oceanic culture history Volume 1*, Pacific Anthropological Records 11, B.P. Bishop Museum, Hawaii.

Hjarno,J. 1967. Maori fish-hooks in southern New Zealand. *Records of the Otago Museum, Anthropology Series* No. 3.

Horwood,L.M. 1989. Trace element analysis of human bone from the prehistoric Moriori of the Chatham Islands with special reference to diet. *Journal of the Royal Society of New Zealand* 19(1):59–71.

Houghton,P. 1980. *The first New Zealanders*. Hodder and Stoughton.

Izquierdo,E.R. 1988. *Contribucion al atlas osteologico de los Teleosteos Ibericos I. dentario y articular*. Ediciones de la Universidad Autonoma de Madrid.

Johannes,R.E. 1981. *Words of the Lagoon*. University of California Press.

Law,R.G. 1972. Archaeology at Harataonga Bay, Great Barrier Island. *Records of the Auckland Institute and Museum* 9:81–123.

Law,R.G. 1975. C14 dates from Harataonga Bay, Great Barrier Island. *New Zealand Archaeological Association Newsletter* 18(1):48–52.

Leach,B.F. 1976. Prehistoric communities in Palliser Bay, New Zealand. Unpublished PhD thesis, Anthropology, University of Otago.

Leach,B.F. 1979. Fish and crayfish from the Washpool Midden site, New Zealand: their use in determining season of occupation and prehistoric fishing methods. *Journal of Archaeological Science* 6:109–126.

Leach,B.F. 1986. A method for analysis of Pacific island fishbone assemblages and an associated data base management system. *Journal of Archaeological Science* 13(2):147–159.

Leach,B.F. 1986. Un cas de chasseurs marins sur une île du Pacifique ? L'analyse ostéologique des restes du kjøkkenmødding à Fa'ahia. *Bulletin de la Société des Études Océaniennes* 19(12):49–53.

Leach,B.F. and Anderson,A.J. 1979. Prehistoric exploitation of crayfish in New Zealand. pp.141–164 In Anderson, A.J. (ed.) *Birds of a Feather*. British Archaeological Reports S62.

Leach,B.F. and Anderson,A.J. 1979. The role of labrid fish in prehistoric economics in New Zealand. *Journal of Archaeological Science* 6(1):1–15.

Leach,B.F. and Davidson,J.M. 1977. Fishing methods and seasonality at Paremata (N160/50). *New Zealand Archaeological Association Newsletter* 20(3):166–175.

Leach,B.F. and Davidson,J.M. 1981. The analysis of fish bone from Kapingamarangi. In Leach,B.F. and Ward,G.K. Archaeology on Kapingamarangi Atoll: a Polynesian outlier in the Eastern Caroline Islands. Privately published by B.F.Leach. pp 114–122.

Leach,B.F. and Davidson,J.M. 1988. The quest for the rainbow runner: prehistoric fishing on Kapingamarangi and Nukuoro atolls, Micronesia. Micronesica 21(1–2):1–22.

Leach,B.F. and Leach,H.M. 1979. (eds) Prehistoric Man in Palliser Bay. National Museum of New Zealand, Bulletin 21.

Leach,B.F. and Manly,B. 1982. Minimum Mahalanobis distance functions and lithic source characterization by multi-element analysis. New Zealand Journal of Archaeology 4:77–109.

Leach,B.F. and Ward,G.K. 1981. Archaeology on Kapingamarangi Atoll: a Polynesian outlier in the Eastern Caroline Islands. Privately published by B.F.Leach.

Leach,B.F. n.d. An anatomical manual for the identification of fishbone from New Zealand archaeological sites. Unpublished manuscript, National Museum of New Zealand.

Leach,B.F. n.d. Unpublished Fishbone Catalogue and Record Books. Unpublished manuscript, National Museum of New Zealand.

Leach,B.F., Anderson,A.J., Sutton,D.G., Bird,J.R., Duerden,P., Clayton,E. 1986. The origin of prehistoric obsidian artefacts from the Chatham and Kermadec islands. New Zealand Journal of Archaeology 8:143–170.

Leach,B.F., Fleming,M., Davidson,J.M., Ward,G.K. and Craib,J. 1988. Prehistoric fishing at Mochong, Rota, Mariana Islands. Man and Culture in Oceania 4:31–62.

Leach,B.F., Intoh,M. and Smith,I.W.G. 1984. Fishing, turtle hunting, and mammal exploitation at Fa'ahia, Huahine, French Polynesia. Journal de la Société des Océanistes 40(79):183–197.

Leach,B.F., Quinn,C., Lyon,G. and Haystead,T. n.d. The frontier of prehistoric economic adaptation in Oceania—the sea. New Zealand Journal of Archaeology, In Press.

Leach,H.M. 1969. Subsistence patterns in prehistoric New Zealand. Studies in Prehistoric Anthropology 2, Otago University.

Leach,H.M. 1976. Horticulture in prehistoric New Zealand. Unpublished PhD thesis, Anthropology, University of Otago.

Leach,H.M. 1979. Evidence of prehistoric gardens in eastern Palliser Bay. In Leach,B.F. and Leach,H.M. (eds), Prehistoric Man in Palliser Bay. National Museum of New Zealand Bulletin 21:137–161.

Leach,H.M. and Hamel,G.E. 1978. The place of Taiaroa Head and other Classic Maori sites in the prehistory of East Otago. Journal of the Royal Society of New Zealand 8(3):239–251.

Leach,H.M. and Hamel,G.E. 1981. Archaic and Classic Maori relationships at Long Beach, Otago: the artefacts and activity areas. New Zealand Journal of Archaeology 3:109–141.

Leach,H.M. and Leach,B.F. 1980. The Riverton site: an archaic adze manufactory in western Southland, New Zealand. New Zealand Journal of Archaeology 2:99–140.

Leahy,A. 1970. Excavations at site N38/30, Motutapu Island, New Zealand. Records of the Auckland Institute and Museum 7:61–82.

Leahy,A. 1972. Further excavations at site N38/30, Motutapu Island, New Zealand. Records of the Auckland Institute and Museum 9:15–26.

Leahy,A. 1974. Excavations at Hot Water Beach (N44/69), Coromandel Peninsula. Records of the Auckland Institute and Museum 11:23–76.

Marshall,Y. 1987. Maori mass capture of freshwater eels: an ethnoarchaeological reconstruction of prehistoric subsistence and social behaviour. New Zealand Journal of Archaeology 9:55–79.

McFadgen,B.G. 1972. Paleoenvironmental studies in the Manawatu sand plain with particular reference to Foxton. Unpublished MA thesis, Anthropology, University of Otago.

McFadgen,B.G. 1980. Maori plaggen soils in New Zealand, their origin and properties. Journal of the Royal Society of New Zealand 10(1):3–19.

McGovern-Wilson,R. 1985. Fiordland National Park, Gazetteer of historic and archaeological sites. Unpublished report to the Department of Lands and Survey, Invercargill.

McIlwraith,M.A. 1976. Archaeology, middens and people. Unpublished MA thesis, Anthropology, University of Otago

Moore,P.R. and Tiller,E.M. 1976. Radiocarbon dates for New Zealand archaeological sites: errata and addenda. *New Zealand Archaeological Association Newsletter* 19(3):151–155.

Norris,B. 1966. Omihi. *Canterbury Museum Archaeological Society Newsletter*, December 1966.

Ollivier,I. 1985. *Extracts from journals relating to the visit to New Zealand in May–June 1772 of the French ships Mascarin and Marquis de Castries under the command of M.-J. Marion du Fresne.* Alexander Turnbull Library, Wellington.

Park,G.S. 1969. Tiwai Point—a preliminary report. *New Zealand Archaeological Association Newsletter* 12(3):143–146.

Paulin,C.D. and Stewart,A.L. 1985. A list of New Zealand teleost fishes held in the National Museum of New Zealand. *National Museum of New Zealand Miscellaneous Series* Number 12.

Paulin,C.D. 1989. Early Maori knowledge of fishes of the New Zealand region, based on an analysis of fish names recorded in the literature. Unpublished paper presented to the Select Committee on the Maori Fisheries Bill.

Piddington,R. 1952. *An introduction to social anthropology.* Oliver and Boyd.

Rowland,M.J. 1978. Investigations of two sites on Slipper Island. *New Zealand Archaeological Association Newsletter* 21(1):31–52.

Scott,S.D. 1970. Excavations at the "Sunde Site", N38/24, Motutapu Island, New Zealand. *Records of the Auckland Institute and Museum* 7:13–30.

Sewell,B. 1988. The fishhook assemblage from the Cross Creek Site (N40/260; T10/399), Sarah's Gully, Coromandel Peninsula, New Zealand. *New Zealand Journal of Archaeology* 10:5–17.

Shawcross,W. 1967. An investigation of prehistoric diet and economy on a coastal site at Galatea Bay, New Zealand. *Proceedings of the Prehistoric Society* 33:107–131.

Shawcross, W. 1972. Energy and ecology: thermodynamic models in archaeology. pp 577-622 In: Clarke, D.L. *Models in archaeology.* Methuen, London.

Simmons,D. 1966. personal commmunication. 12 Minto Street, Remuera, Auckland.

Sinclair,E.D. 1977. Interim report of salvage excavation at Paremata—(N160/50). *New Zealand Archaeological Association Newsletter* 20(3):151–165.

Skinner,H.D. and Baucke,W. 1928. *The Morioris.* Memoirs of the Bishop Museum 9(5).

Smith,I.W.G. 1976. Prehistoric fur seal exploitation on the southwest coast of Chatham Island. BA Hons Dissertation, Anthropology, University of Otago. Also circulated as Working Papers in Chatham Islands archaeology № 7.

Smith,I.W.G. 1985. Sea mammal hunting and prehistoric subsistence in New Zealand. Unpublished PhD Dissertation, Anthropology, University of Otago.

Smith,I.W.G. 1986. Changes in New Zealand distribution of the Southern Fur Seal. Appendix 2. *Journal of the Polynesian Society* 95:337–338.

Strickland,R. 1989. Nga Tini a Tangaroa. Manuscript, MAFFish, Rotorua.

Sutton,D.G. 1977. Radiocarbon dates from the Chatham Islands–II. *New Zealand Archaeological Association Newsletter* 20(2):127.

Sutton,D.G. 1979. Polynesian coastal hunters in the sub-antarctic zone: a case for the recognition of convergent cultural adaptation. Unpublished PhD dissertation, Anthropology, University of Otago.

Sutton,D.G. 1986. Maori demographic change, 1769–1840. *Journal of the Polynesian Society* 95:291–339.

Sutton,D.G. 1989. Moriori fishing: intensive exploitation of the inshore zone. *In* Sutton, D.G. (ed.) *Saying so doesn't make it so. Papers in honour of B.Foss Leach.* New Zealand Archaeological Association Monograph 17, pp 116–131.

Sutton,D.G. and Marshall,Y.M. 1980. Coastal hunting in the subantarctic zone. *New Zealand Journal of Archaeology* 2:25–50.

Terrell,J. 1967. Galatea Bay—the exavation of a beach-stream midden site on Ponui Island in the Hauraki Gulf, New Zealand. *Transactions of the Royal Society of New Zealand (General)* 2(3):31–70.

Till,M. 1984. Seasonality in prehistoric Murihiku: the evidence from oxygen isotope ratios. Unpublished MA thesis, Anthropology, University of Otago.

Tregear,E. 1891. *The Maori-Polynesian comparative dictionary.* Humanities Press.

Trotter,M.M. 1966. *In Canterbury Museum Archaeological Society Newsletter,* September 1966.

Trotter,M.M. 1974. *Archaeological investigations at Takahanga, Kaikoura.* Canterbury Museum, Christchurch.

Trotter,M.M. 1977. *Titirangi archaeology: an interim report.* Marlborough Sounds Maritime Park Board, Blenheim.

Trotter,M.M. 1980. Archaeological investigations at Avoca Point, Kaikoura. *Records of Canterbury Museum* 9(4):277–288.

Trotter,M.N. 1982. Canterbury and Marlborough. *In* N.Prickett (ed.), *The first thousand years: regional perspectives in New Zealand archaeology.* New Zealand Archaeological Association Monograph 13, Dunmore Press, Palmerston North:83–102.

Walls,J.Y. 1979. Salvage at The Glen—a late Archaic site in Tasman Bay. *New Zealand Archaeological Association Newsletter* 22(1):6–19.

www.ingramcontent.com/pod-product-compliance
Lightning Source LLC
Chambersburg PA
CBHW051307270326
41926CB00030B/4761